Penguin Books
No – Honestly!

CHARLOTTE BINGHAM wrote her first book,
Coronet Among the Weeds, when she was nineteen.
It was published as an autobiography, and shortly
afterwards she married TERENCE BRADY with
whom she has written in partnership for eight years.
They have contributed to many successful television
series, including *Take Three Girls*, and *Upstairs
Downstairs*. It is upon the second volume of
Charlotte Bingham's autobiography *Coronet Among
the Grass* that they have based their current
television series.

Charlotte Bingham

No – Honestly!

Penguin Books

Penguin Books Ltd, Harmondsworth,
Middlesex, England
Penguin Books Inc., 7110 Ambassador Road,
Baltimore, Maryland 21207, U.S.A.
Penguin Books Australia Ltd, Ringwood,
Victoria, Australia
Penguin Books Canada Ltd, 41 Steelcase Road West,
Markham, Ontario, Canada
Penguin Books (N.Z.) Ltd, 182–190 Wairau Road,
Auckland 10, New Zealand

First published separately as
Coronet Among the Weeds (1963) and
Coronet Among the Grass (1972) by
William Heinemann Ltd
Published as *No – Honestly!* in Penguin Books 1974

Copyright © Charlotte Bingham, 1963, 1972

Made and printed in Great Britain by
Hunt Barnard Printing Ltd, Aylesbury, Bucks
Set in Linotype Plantin

Contents

Dear Reader,

Clara has forced me to set pen to paper, in order to explain to you precisely what is contained in this volume. (No, Clara, I won't forget to tell them that the first book was written when you were a teenager, and that you've changed a lot since then, no matter what your Auntie Herbert says.)

I'm sorry. Where was I? Yes, so the first book is the one about Clara as a teenager, and the second one is her slightly biased account of our marriage, upon which the London Weekend Television series *No – Honestly* is based. Now I'm going to quickly sign off before Clara has time for another of her interruptions. I mean, there just isn't the space. No, Honestly.

C.D.

Coronet Among the Weeds

I

I was thinking in bed the other night I must have been out with nearly three hundred men, and I still haven't found a superman. I don't know what a superman is, but I know there must be one somewhere. So does Migo. Migo's my girl friend, she's a good thing. She's not soppy, but she agrees with me that somewhere there must be a superman. Actually I think most girls believe in a superman. I mean they don't really believe all that phoney stuff you hear them jazzing on about. You know, like girls who look you dead pan in the face drawing nervously on a cigarette and come out with that corny line about men only wanting 'one thing'. That's when they're about seventeen and when you meet them a couple of years later they're still dragging nervously at their cigarettes, but carrying on about their careers.

Then you get the ones who go on about parties, and spend the whole time asking you if you know people or if you're going somewhere for the weekend. It's like parties are a sort of nervous habit with them. And the way they go on about knowing people. You can't know everyone. They're like that nutty saint who wanted to empty the sea into his sandpit. No, hell, I've got it wrong. It was this angel who was scooping up the sea and emptying it into his sandpit, and this saint told him, 'You'll never do it boy.' Someone ought to tell them. Anyway both these types of girls anyone with half an eye can see are just waiting around for a superman; and they don't even let themselves know, but they are.

Actually I think what a Frenchman once said to me is true. He said all little girls were born women. And when I think, I can remember flirting with a boy friend of my aunt's when I was four. I think he had something really. But most girls don't get around to really thinking about a superman till they're about thirteen.

I started playing the 'other woman' role when I was thirteen. We had a Swedish maid. Honestly you wouldn't have known she was Swedish, she was like a huge Spanish woman or something. With black hair and a huge bronzed body, and she had this boy friend called Mess. Yes, honestly he was called Mess. He said it was short for a Persian name. He was Persian. Anyway he spoke English with an American accent and wore denim jeans, and my grandmother set the dogs on him every time she saw him hanging round our gate. She doesn't like foreigners. Actually she doesn't like many people. My brother says, if they're not Jews or Germans or Negroes, then they're Strangers and that's just as bad. She's always going on about 'all those filthy disgusting people', and it's no good telling her she's one of them because she won't believe you.

Anyway, this Mess: our Swede was mad about him. She used to lie around on our lawn in a *broderie anglaise* bikini hoping he'd get by the dogs and my grandmother. My mother used to make her take me to Brighton for the day, and Mess used to meet us off the train and we'd go and have coffee with him. I used to have an awful time keeping him from seeing my profile. I had a complex about not having a chin. It was maddening because this Swede had one. And I used to get a stiff neck trying not to turn my head, but anyway it was quite fun. And then I read if you tied a scarf under your chin at night it helped, and honestly I think it made a difference because it's not too bad now. Also I used to tie my hands on to the rail above my head so all the blood drained from them and they looked dead-white and aristocratic. It was quite a business getting into bed.

Anyway Mess used to walk to the bus-stop with us, and then he and this Swede would start kissing. Honestly, you've never seen anything like it. I timed them once, two and a half minutes for one kiss. I don't know if that's a record, but it's not bad. She must have had good lungs that girl.

Then Mess started going to London during the week and just coming back for weekends, and sometimes our Swede couldn't get the weekend off so she used to send me to see him with letters.

10

I don't think she was very intelligent. He had a room in a house down the road, and we used to play his gramophone, and he'd say I had pretty hair, but I had hell keeping him from seeing my profile.

The thing is, I didn't particularly think he was attractive, but I wanted to see if I could win him from that Swede and her chin. Only for fun, to sort of see if I could do it. It wasn't malicious or anything. So, anyhow, she used to go and see him in London sometimes during the week, and she always asked me what she should wear and how she should do her hair and everything. So one day I got a bit bored and I told her she looked wonderful with her hair all flat, and wearing this thick black dress. So she went to London like that. Honestly, I don't think she could have been very intelligent. 'Course Mess told her she looked awful, and sent her back by the next train. Actually it wasn't much fun after that because the Swede went back to Sweden, and the whole thing lost its point, but anyway it was quite interesting.

After the Swede went back to Sweden, we moved back to London. No, just before we moved back to London I went to my first dance. It was hell, honestly. No one wanted to dance with me because I was thirteen and they were all fifteen, and they kept on doing these Scottish reels and everything. And my parents were there, and my father kept winking at me as if it didn't matter, but it did, so I went into the kitchen and talked to the dogs. At least they didn't have spots like half those damn boys. It's a funny thing about dogs when you're young. You feel much more for your dog than most of your relations. Except your grandfather or something. I know more girls who start crying about their dogs and their grandfathers than anything else.

Anyway after that dance I swore I'd go back to that place when I was fifteen and make everyone mad to dance with me. Funny thing actually because I did.

When we moved back to London we stopped having maids because the house was too small, and I spent most of the time at the movies with my cousin. I was fat and she had spots so we had plenty to talk about. Then my mother said I should go to dancing classes. They were hell too, no kidding. All these boys looking at you, and this man banging away on the piano and this

11

woman pushing you in and out of eightsomes and things. Then you had to pretend to be things. Or run up and down pretending you'd got a nightie on. Honestly, try running up and down pretending you've got a nightie on with a whole lot of boys of fifteen sneering at you. And they had such awful faces. And they were either terribly tall or absolutely tiny. So you spent the whole time walking backwards talking to the bottom button on a jacket, or the top of a small greasy head. Honestly, it was murder.

Then a girl at school's mother started getting up this Charity Dance. And everyone decided to go, and my mother said she'd give a buffet supper beforehand. I didn't know any boys, so my mother asked a friend of her's son, and my cousin asked a boy she knew when she was four. I didn't have a dress so we had one made at the dressmaker and my mother bought me some flowers to pin on my shoulder, and I was a bit thinner. When they all arrived the boys turned out to be rather a good thing. Even my cousin's friend whom she hadn't seen since she was four. Rather a lucky strike really.

Then what the hell do you think happened? This girl's boy-friend got measles. Least he rang up and said he had measles, and she just turned up without anybody. Honestly, it was absolutely typical. Just because she was two years older than all of us and madly swoony she knew she was okay, thank you. If anyone was going to sit out it wasn't going to be pussy old her. She wasn't even the sort of girl you could like much. She went round madly pretending she wasn't swoony, but still, a terrible lot of people thought she was awfully nice. Especially men.

Anyhow I did all right at the dance until the eightsome started up, and suddenly everyone had partners except me. And that girl was looking coy with my partner. So I had to go and sit behind a pillar on one of those ghastly gilt chairs. And when it stopped and I started to jump up and rush back to claim a partner, some fiendish voice shouted encore and it started all over again. I swear it was that girl. Honestly there was nothing she wouldn't stop at, really there wasn't, she even came up and apologized afterwards. And she used to take all these girls around with her to parties and introduce them to boys and say how clever they were to these boys, and of course these boys would never look at them again; they'd just swoon round her saying they were terribly glad she wasn't clever.

Except for that damn eightsome, the dance was quite fun. Afterwards we all arranged to go to a movie the next day. This boy who was my partner stayed the night with us because he lived in Surrey. He ate up all the trifles from the night before for breakfast. My mother was awfully pleased, and she thought he had nice manners. I liked him too but he didn't make me swoon. You know. It was this other girl's partner I liked. We all did actually. He had one of those boy-next-door faces. He was there when we went to the movies, but this girl sat next to him until the elastic in her knickers went and she had to go to the loo and find a safety-pin. Then I moved up and sat next to him. We were both laughing because it was quite funny, and he said, 'Are you going to the rugger match tomorrow?' and I said, 'No.'

I didn't see him again after that until the Easter holidays when me and this girl got asked to a dance by the daughter of a friend of my mother. We had to take our own partners, so she brought this boy-next-door type and I didn't know anyone I wanted to bring so I didn't take anyone.

The dance was in a sort of hall, and there was a band and a friend of my mother's played the drums. He was damned good actually. Anyway I didn't have a partner so I had to dance with this boy called George. Honestly it was terrible. He had glasses and his hair came up to my chin; he was much worse than any-thing I'd met at the dancing classes. And he just couldn't dance. I mean, he couldn't even do a straight walk in time to the music, and we had to do this shuffle up and down because he couldn't manage the corners. And this other girl was having a fabulous time with her old boy-next-door type, whirling by because he danced absolutely marvellously, and they kept on smiling at me so I had to pretend George was my dream come true.

Then the other girl was asked to dance by someone else and the boy-next-door type came up and asked me to dance. We danced a waltz and then the lights went out and he whirled me about in the candlelight and he kissed my cheek just before the lights went up. I nearly died it was so romantic. Then George

13

came up and asked me for my address and 'I gave it to him just to show the boy-next-door type he wasn't the only thing around.

Do you know that stupid ass wrote to me. I didn't get many letters, so of course my mother wanted to know who had written to me. I just said it was from a girl. You wouldn't believe it, but he wrote to me at school too. All about him playing squash. It made me sick to think of him playing squash, bouncing up and down and sweating. My cousin laughed her head off though; she said I should keep the letter, but I just couldn't bear to. It made me sick.

I forgot about the corney old boy-next-door type after two different girls told me they were swooning about him in the cloakroom. I hate obvious men. When girls go on about a man being attractive he never is. He's just stomping round *being* madly attractive. You know: 'Here's super old me. Now swoon everyone.' Of course some girls finds everyone attractive. No, honestly, they really do. It's not the anything-in-trousers technique, they really think all these types are swoony. My mother says her sister's like that. She says she tells my mother she's got the most super young man coming to dinner, and a bottle-nosed man of forty comes in. Rather sad really.

After that the most awful thing happened. I got this nervous reaction about this uncle of mine. Least he's not a real uncle, he's an uncle by marriage. He's frightfully nice actually. But God it was boring having this nervous reaction. I wasn't in love with him or anything, I just went this awful colour every time he came into the room or said something. A friend of mine had the same thing, only she went this colour every time anyone at all looked at her. So we used to do this thing. Every time we felt a blush coming on we'd look at something white. It really helped; honestly it was fantastic. I still do it sometimes, even now.

Well, me and this girl kept on having bets about things. You know:

'Bet you I get a bra before you do.'

'Bet you I'm engaged before you are.'

And so on. Anyway she'd won on the bra stakes. She had a bigger bust than me. So I was absolutely determined to be kissed before she was. Only it's not so damned easy, because you've got to get someone to kiss you. It didn't count if you went up and kissed them. Well, we were all at this curry party a girl friend gave in her flat. And we sat around on the floor eating curry and wearing jeans and shirts and things. Then everyone started sort of dancing a bit, and this boy in a kilt did a Highland-fling in the hall.

But I just went on dancing with this same boy all the time, because I knew if you wanted someone to kiss you, you had to dance with him the whole evening. I didn't like dancing with just one person, but I wanted to win this bet. I'd got quite good at talking to people by then. I mean I didn't feel shy or anything, and I think he rather liked me. I quite liked him actually, and he didn't have spots or anything. I did draw the line at being kissed the first time by someone with spots. I mean you can take betting too far.

Anyway they switched the corney old light off for the last dance, and he said,

'Can I kiss you?'

And I said,

'All right.'

So he did.

I was jolly disappointed. I don't know what I expected to happen, but it was so dull. Honestly, I remember thinking what a lot of fuss people made about nothing. He kissed me again by the back door after he'd driven me home. I thought I'd better let him, though I didn't like it much, but anyway I won that bet.

Then this boy called Mervyn whom I'd met at the dancing classes rang me up and asked me to this party. He just said it was a party so I put on a sort of party dress and flowers in my hair, and me and a girl friend went to his flat. She was wearing a party dress too. When we arrived at his flat we rang the bell but nothing happened, so I pushed the door and it opened. So I said,

'Let's go in.'

It was one of those flats with long expensive corridors. You know. You wouldn't know you were walking the carpets are so thick. The only way you can tell is that your legs keep moving.

Anyway we walked along these corridors, and kept peering in and out of different rooms, but they were all just terribly quiet and expensive. Then we got to the end of this corridor and we heard a gramophone going, so we went in. And it was terribly dark, nothing but a few candles. I was a bit scared and I said,

'Shall we go?'

But this other girl said,

'No, hell let's stay and see what happens.'

I couldn't help thinking about my mother. She gets a bit conventional sometimes. I didn't think it was her sort of party. But we found Mervyn, and he was a bit drunk, but he introduced us to these other friends of his who were quite nice, and we all danced a bit, and I didn't feel so nervous. And there was a boy sitting in a corner reading a book and laughing, and they all asked if I'd read it. I hadn't. So they said I should, it was a frightfully vulgar book someone had bought in Paris. But I said I didn't want to. Honestly I'm not a prude, but I hate that awful commercial-traveller attitude. You know: it *must* be funny because it's vulgar. Actually I think the English are rather awful like that. Anyway this boy called Mervyn kept on giving me these drinks that tasted just like lemonade, but I realized they couldn't be when I started feeling dizzy. I said to the boy I was dancing with,

'I feel a bit drunk.'

And he said,

'You look a bit drunk.'

So I went and looked in the mirror, and I looked awful. The flowers were hanging off their kirby grip, and someone had spilt something on my dress. I said to this boy,

'Maybe I'll feel better when I've had something to eat.'

But he said, why didn't I try walking in a straight line, he'd help me. I just couldn't do it. So they got this other boy and they all helped me along very slowly, but I looked so funny that we kept on giggling. All the time, though, I kept on wondering what my mother would say if she saw me. It was some thought. Honestly, she'd have had a fit. Then Mervyn started throwing glasses at the wall. I think he must have felt insecure or something. He just kept on picking up these glasses and throwing them at the wall. There was nothing wrong with the glasses, he just kept on breaking them. Mind you, his parents were divorced.

I went up to him, and he stopped throwing glasses, and I said I wanted to go home and thank you for the lovely party. But he said I couldn't possibly go home, I must come to this night club he knew. I said I didn't like night clubs. Actually I'd never been in one. He said I would adore this one, so everyone got into a taxi, and I had to go too because I didn't have the taxi money to take me home. When we arrived, there wasn't enough money for everyone to go in, but I wasn't going to miss seeing inside now I was there, so six of us went in with Mervyn. It was as corney as anything inside. Honestly, all that money, and there wasn't any decent vice anywhere. It was just rather dark and there was this old band playing away, and a lot of old men sitting around with women and drinking and eating. And a few of them were creeping up and down the floor with these stupid-looking blondes. And that was all. Still it made something to talk about at school.

Then Migo and I decided to give a party. We made up a rhyming invitation, sitting on the radiator at school, and she typed it out on cards with one of the nuns' typewriters. They looked rather good and we knew a lot of people by then, what with the dancing classes and things. My mother said we could have the party in our house. She spent days putting nuts on trifles and cheese in celery and things, and we put the food in the dining-room downstairs and kept the drawing-room for dancing and asked this woman in to wash up. All the parents went off for the evening as soon as they saw everyone arriving. We had this huge bowl of punch in the drawing-room and rock-and-roll records.

Actually it was quite gay. Everyone started dancing and playing these games where you have to stand on a matchbox with a name written on your back and try and find someone to match the name on your back. Then whoever finds the person that matches them, without getting off the matchbox, wins. I went down to the kitchen when they started passing grapefruits under their chins. There was this woman washing up.

'The floor's going to give in,' she said.

I looked at the ceiling, and it did look a bit bendy.

2

'It oughtn't to be allowed,' she said.

She wasn't very nice. And she had this nervous tic. She kept on licking her finger and pushing at her forehead with it. Like one of those fly-catching frogs with long tongues.

I went upstairs with more glasses, and they'd all started dancing in our garden. It's not very big, but anyway they did. And do you know it was fantastic the next morning. There wasn't a single thing growing there. It gave my father a bit of a shock I can tell you. Honestly, one moment he was looking for greenfly and the next he was just standing around with all this earth.

'Your father's very hurt,' my mother said.

It's always much worse if they're hurt. I think she knows that.

'A friend of mine broke the punch-bowl,' I said.

'Are you sure he's a friend?' she said. She can be rather sarcastic sometimes. The drawing-room smelt like a pub for weeks, but I think everyone enjoyed themselves.

Well, the thing was what with one thing and another I was nearly sixteen by this time. So my mother said I should leave school. She doesn't believe in girls knowing a frightful lot or going to university. She says they're mucky, the rooms of girls who go to university, I mean. She just thinks girls should have a bit of culture, and know how to cook and keep things clean. Actually I don't know if she isn't right sometimes. I mean all those damn suffragettes and things, no one gets up for you on the tube now. I think it must have been quite fun when women were rather mysterious, and men didn't know all about them. Look at the end-product of women being free. I mean, go on, look at it. It's a poor old career girl sitting in her digs wondering whether she ought to ring up her boy-friend or not. It makes you wonder sometimes.

Anyway my mother said she thought I ought to leave school. The nuns didn't want me to, but she did. So I did. I was jolly sad to leave school actually. I went to the most super convent. All the nuns were marvellous; honestly they were the most broadminded people you've ever met. I get very cross about nuns. People always go on and on about them not knowing anything and shutting themselves away from Life and all that stuff. Like the saints. I get cross about them too. For heaven's sake the way people go on you'd think it was easy to be a saint. I bet if you met a saint he'd make Wyatt Earp look like a weed. Really, they had to be frightfully tough.

Migo, this girl friend of mine, went to this convent too. She left when she was sixteen with me. She wanted to go to Paris. We both did. We used to sit about and talk about it, and make up the most marvellous things that were going to happen to us. But this nun asked Migo if she thought she had a vocation. Honestly, she really thought Migo would make a good nun. We couldn't get over it. I remember I was so stunned I kept asking her if it was true. I ask you, Migo a nun. They never asked me if I wanted to be a nun. I don't think I ever showed any tendencies actually. Most girls do. I remember I once asked my mother what she'd do if I became a nun, and she said I couldn't possibly, it was too expensive. She's quite holy, but you have to give them this lump sum when you go in, and we never seem to have lump sums.

Actually I don't think that nun could have known Migo very well. Anyone can see she's just looking for a superman.

2

Just before I went to Paris with Migo, I fell in love. It was the older man routine. Though he wasn't all that old actually, but he was a grown-up and I wasn't. I didn't like it much, being in love I mean. But I was quite resigned. It's just one of those things you have to go through, like teething or something. I fell in love with him for a funny reason. It sounds stupid. But he didn't flirt with me or anything. And he had the most innocent eyes. I know it sounds soppy for a man, but they were really innocent. 'Course he was amusing and good looking too, but that was the main reason, this sort of innocence I mean.

He was an actor, and he was staying with us till he got a flat. He used to rehearse in his room, and I would sit on the stairs for hours listening to him. That's the thing about being in love, you find yourself doing nutty things, and you don't even think they're nutty. I knew a girl once who was madly in love with a married man, and she used to stand outside his house with her mother's hats on, waiting for his wife to go out. She didn't want the wife to know what she looked like. I said, didn't it get a bit boring, and she said, yes, but it was worth it.

It's pretty funny living in the same house as someone you're in love with. I used to have breakfast and everything with this actor, and sit on the kitchen stairs and talk. And he used to lend me his after-shave lotion to stop my mother smelling when my dogs made pools on the carpets.

Migo and I had to go by train to Paris because of my luggage. My mother's got funny ideas about luggage. I once watched her packing for a weekend. She kept walking round her room muttering and putting clothes in suitcases.

'I must take my gold lamé for drinks, and my blue for dinner, and six jumpers because the heating's so bad, and my tweed in case we beagle.'

'You don't know how to beagle,' I said. But she said you never knew.

Even when I'd gone to Paris she never stopped sending me parcels with more clothes and medicines in them. She made me swear on the family Bible, that my aunt's poodle chewed up, that I wouldn't buy French medicines and to send her a telegram if I was ill. When I was ill, they never gave me anything but suppositories. Honestly whatever you had wrong with you they just said,

'*Ah-ha, il faut les suppositoires.*'

Nothing much happened on the journey to Paris except someone was sick down my coat. I told my mother when I rang her after we arrived, but she wasn't interested. She was annoyed about this person not waiting till they got to the loo. She said there was no excuse, you could always feel it coming on, and really it was too annoying all down my nice new coat.

I was staying with a Marquis in Paris. A very nice Marquis actually, with six children and a very old flat near the Pont des Arts. They were demoneyed aristocrats like my family. Only I think we enjoy it more than they did. I think you either do or you don't. I know my mother's jolly relieved; she says she couldn't have stood all those draughty castles. But some people miss them – their castles I mean – they sit about and regret them and talk about their ancestors. Ancestors are hell's boring. I've had to sit through eveningfuls of them. It's all right if there are lots of people, because they all talk quite happily about their own, and no one listens. Like when everyone starts talking about their fillings. They all have their fingers in their mouths pointing out their fillings so no one listens to anyone else, but they're quite happy. But, if you get only a couple of people telling you about the Battle of Bilsworth Common, you've got to listen. Then sure as hell they'll suddenly find they're related and go all the way back to the Black Death, and you've had it.

Migo was staying with a family of Communists. She said they weren't at all bad, they just kept on going on about Moscow. Everything in Moscow was marvellous, rather like the Irish and the Old Country. Migo got a bit bored of Moscow at every meal, so she said, why didn't they go and live there if it was so marvellous. They said, no, they weren't rats to desert a sinking ship, they preferred to fight for Communism in Paris. What I said to Migo was, I bet they'd get browned off if all the women in Paris looked like the women in Moscow. I bet they would too.

Migo said that except for Moscow they were quite nice. Amusing too, which is unusual for Communists really. On the whole they're a bit inclined to be po-faced. When I was about fourteen I got a bit atheistic, so I thought I'd have a go at being a Communist. My mother was frightful squashing. She said I'd never be any good, I was far too happy and washed too much. And I hadn't got a grudge. Apparently it's no good unless you've got a grudge.

A friend of Migo's told us about these lectures for foreigners at the Sorbonne, so we went along and enrolled. I don't know if you know what the Sorbonne looks like inside, but they have this enormous room like the Roman Forum with tiers of seats, and the lecturer stands in the middle on a dais. We were fascinated by all the types that went to these lectures. Absolutely every nationality you can think of. The Americans took down screeds of notes, but the Chinese never had a piece of paper on them, they just had brains like tape-recorders that sucked everything in. One Chinese I used to sit next to, would just gracefully close his eyes when the lecture started and sit immobile till it ended, then he would open them and look inscrutable.

The first week we were there, a man stood on his head during one of the lectures. Everyone began to laugh, because being in a lecture is rather like being in church; anything seems funny. I asked Migo what he was doing, and she said he was either a Yogi or a beatnik. I was awfully pleased I hadn't missed him, because he was the first one I'd ever seen. I'd led a bit of a sheltered life, what with one thing and another.

I got to know the French quite well living with this French family. They're different from the English. They cook, talk a lot, and don't wash much. They're more intelligent than the English because they never stop taking exams. They start when they're five, then just never stop. And they spend the whole time asking each other about them: when they're going to take them, how they're going to do them, whether they passed, why they failed, when the next one is. It's a sort of social game really. The French have a lot of social games. And they have all these rules about what you can say *dans le salon* and what you can't say *dans le salon*. You don't have to be *dans le salon* not to be able to say these things you're not meant to, you can be anywhere. But you just can't say them. There's not much you can say actually, except how's aunt Ag and the weather and stuff. Migo didn't have trouble with *le salon* because of being with Communists. *Le salon* is absolutely not on with Communists.

I never had a bath the whole time I was in Paris. The thing was they had a bath but, if you turned on the taps, the ceiling fell down, so there wasn't much point. I didn't mind not having a bath, but I got a guilt complex about not washing. I spent the whole time thinking I was dirty and standing in a bucket of water. It was stupid, because not many people wash when they have a bath. I know my father doesn't. He just thinks and has a bit of a rest. Though not if my mother can help it. As soon as she knows he's in there she remembers that she's left half her things behind, or she wants to tell him something frightfully important. Then she starts knocking on the door and shouting, but he turns on the taps and pretends he can't hear. Don't blame him really.

I had quite a hard time learning French, because I'm not intelligent. It's funny because everyone else in my family is. But they always say your children take after someone obscure. It makes me a bit nervous when I look at some of my relations. My mother kept on hoping I'd be intelligent, but I was a disappointment. The first school I went to they had this old Montessori method, where you only do what you want to do. It didn't work on me because of not being intelligent. I just had this idea it was more fun to play than to work, and didn't learn to read till I was six.

As soon as I did speak a little French, I started to go to French dances, but I didn't have much success with Frenchmen as long as they knew I was English. They weren't very keen on English girls. Luckily I don't look very English, because I had one grandfather who was French, so they often got let in for something they hadn't bargained for. But they couldn't stand it for long. So I wrote myself a French dance-type conversation, timed it to last half an hour and learnt it off by heart. It turned out to be a jolly good thing. I'd just dance away quite happily having this conversation then I'd change partners and start all over again. They all said what a marvellous accent I had and you'd never think I was English, and I'd tell them about this French grandfather of mine, and they'd say, ah, that explained everything. They even thought I was witty.

One thing about Frenchmen though. They can dance. Which is more than Englishmen can. Englishmen scoop you up if you're small like me and press you against the side of their ear, and leave you there for the rest of the evening. I once saw a girl scooped right out of her dress, only this nit who'd scooped her was holding her so tight that neither of them could see what had happened.

There was a Count I danced a lot with in Paris, and he used to take me to the movies, and teach me French *argot*. French *argot* is much more fun than *le salon* French. I got a bit muddled sometimes, and I told a Duchess that I thought French tarts were excellent. It was a bit embarrassing I can tell you. Actually French tarts look jollier than English ones. I had a friend who lived next door to a few. She said they were always singing and laughing and things. Except for one who was called Jeannette la Noire. She was always dressed in black and had long dyed black hair and she never smiled, just played the violin. Of course my mother says that tarts with a heart of gold are a myth. But my grandfather used to say that some of the nicest people he knew were tarts. What my grandmother wanted to know was how he knew. But my mother says that it was different in his day, and you don't get such a good class of girl nowadays. Of course peak tart-time was the Regency days, there's no doubt about that. They had a much better time than the wives, and influence over the old Iron Duke and people.

Migo didn't go to many dances, because her Communists didn't have much social life. She said they used to have men in mackintoshes coming to see them at midnight, but none of them seemed to give dances. So she joined a students' society which gave parties in a cellar, and stately-home visits once a fortnight on Thursdays.

The cellar parties could be quite fun because a lot of Sorbonne people went, and they had a jazz band. The Marquis's wife didn't approve of students or cellars, so I just used to tell her I was doing a cultural course on Eastern philosophy. There were a lot of quite cultured Arabs about so I didn't think it was much of a lie. A friend of mine called Daphne fell in love with one of them. She wanted to marry him and go back to Arabia with him and everything. I thought it was a good idea. My favourite saint tried to convert the Arabs. He only ever converted one, and he went back to being a Mohammedan as soon as this old saint was dead. That's why he was my favourite saint. Also he lived it up like anything before he started being a saint.

Daphne didn't marry her Arab in the end actually. She said he wasn't genuine enough. He didn't have a camel or wear robes or live in a tent or anything. The Arab was furious when she stopped going out with him. He went round telling everyone it was because he was an Arab and she was prejudiced. It wasn't that at all; she just stopped being in love with him. But he wouldn't believe her.

Some of the cellar parties could get a bit wild. Beatniks got too hep and started throwing things. Sometimes it wasn't too dangerous, but if they really went potty all the girls had to lock themselves in the loos till they calmed down a bit. It was rather boring sitting in the loos but it was better than nothing. We made up stories and shouted them over the top at each other, because you can't play hopscotch or anything much in a loo it's too small. Occasionally I climbed over the top and had a look at one of the others, but mostly we just told these stories till everyone had quietened down a bit. Once I climbed over to see a girl and she started crying.

'It's all right this always happens, they soon stop,' I said.

But she just kept on crying and saying,

'I'm *au pair*!'

'We'll think up a super excuse, don't worry,' I said.

But she just kept on saying it was all right for me but she

was *au pair*, so in the end I got back into my own loo again. There wasn't much I could do.

I thought she was a bit soppy crying, but you had to feel sorry for her. Honestly being *au pair* in France is *pas un joke*. It sounds all right, that's the trouble. What usually happens is you get this poor girl who wants to learn French, but doesn't want to go to finishing-school. So all her relations and friends write off to people they know, and eventually someone comes up with a frightfully posh family who have millions of servants and just want someone to speak a few words of English to one of their nine children for two hours every morning. Of course this poor creature arrives with dreams of gallant Frenchmen paying her court, only to find that she's washing up till midnight, and the only Frenchman around is old Monsieur wheezing away at supper every night. One of Migo's cousins went *au pair* to look after a girl of fifteen. She had to speak English to this drip in the morning, walk her in the afternoons, and get this – give her a bath at night. Honestly, she was really meant to bath this huge great girl every night, wash behind her ears for her and everything. She went on strike after a bit, she really couldn't stand it. She said the girl's feet were so big.

Except for the old Count and a few French types I met at dances, I didn't have many boy-friends. Migo and I mostly went around with a mixed bunch of people. There were some English cads, and a lot of pre-deb type girls who went around behaving badly with various weeds. They really were weeds these boys, anyone could see they were. I couldn't understand these girls swooning over them; I don't think they were in love with them. They were just bored. Nothing to do so they let these weeds drool over them. I can't understand people going on like that. I mean, okay super if you're in love with somebody, but just any old drip because you've got nothing better to do – I don't get it honestly I don't. I mean you should have *seen* some of them. Not even the cat would have brought them in. And they used to do it all over the place. You couldn't even go to the movies, and you'd look down the row after five minutes and everyone was locked in someone else's arms. Anyway Migo said it was unhygienic.

There was this girl called Jennifer like that. She was really embarrassing with these complete weeds.

'Do you like them making love to you?' I asked her once.

She gave me a deep look, then said, 'No.'

'Well, why do you let them?' I said.

'If you'd had a father like mine, you'd know why,' she said.

'What did he do to you?'

'He gave me an inferiority complex.'

'What's that got to do with weeds making love to you?'

'I don't feel so inferior,' she said.

One or two girls went Latin Quarter all in capital letters. They weren't very good at it, but anyway they did. You know: grew their hair, dyed it and didn't wash. It would have been all right if they'd been amusing, but they weren't. They just slept with a few beards and went round talking about it rather loudly, pretty boring really. I mean it's not as if it's difficult.

I suppose youthful impressions of Paris are corney. Actually I suppose Paris is rather corney. I didn't think so. Even accidents were fun. Everyone shouted happily, the whole boulevard stopped and took sides, then they all went home to lunch and discussed it over the *pâté*. There was one thing that was a bore though, and that was being hooted by men. It's not a compliment, because they just stop and shout at anything when they're not in a hurry. Most of the time Migo and I didn't really mind, we'd just hum a little tune and pretend it wasn't happening. But every now and then we'd get dead tired of it, so I'd shut one eye and limp, and Migo would help me along looking very po. It always worked. They wouldn't whistle or anything, just pass us by looking rather sad.

We went round one or two of the old monuments, and the Louvre and all that. It was okay if I went with Migo or somebody, but every now and then the Marquis's wife would arrange for one of the daughters to go with me, and that was hell. They were a bit serious about culture, specially the Egyptians, and there were all these mummies in the Louvre. Genuine ones all right, but they all looked the same to me, so I'd take a few peppermints in with me and sit on a mummy till it was time to go home.

I liked the art galleries though. I've always wanted to draw, but I've never been any good. At school I had a cart-horse fixation. I never stopped drawing these nine-legged cart-horses everywhere, I don't know why. Anyway, my favourite art gallery was the one with all the Impressionists in it. I liked Toulouse-Lautrec one of the best. He was fantastic that man, he really was. He could draw all these things like prostitutes waiting for a medical, and lesbians in bed, but he never made you feel sick. You just thought they were sad and funny and everything. It meant quite a lot to me being able to look at those pictures actually; because, though I knew about lesbians and people, it still hurt to think about them.

There was one picture of a woman that made me cry. Mind you, anything made me cry then. Honestly I couldn't even see a beggar in the Métro and I'd start crying all over the place. Anyway this picture made me cry because this woman had sad feet, they really were the saddest feet you've ever seen, with shoes with droopy rosettes on them. Whenever I was bored I'd go and sit in front of these feet and cry, and when the actor I was in love with came to Paris for a few days I was dying to show him. I kept on going on about this picture, and eventually he got to see it.

Do you know, he didn't like it. It nearly killed me, don't ask me why, but it did. I mean it didn't matter that he didn't like it, he was nice enough without having to like this picture too, but I still went on minding about him not liking it. I told someone about it afterwards, and they said it was one of the facts of life. You just can't share everything with your superman. You have to tell yourself they're super, and forget the rest.

It was jolly nice when that actor came to Paris actually. We didn't do much, just walked around and looked at everything. We didn't talk much either, come to think of it, or make love or anything. It doesn't sound very exciting, but it was. I cried when he went, and all those drips made me feel sick for weeks afterwards. That's the trouble when you do meet a superman. Everyone else makes you feel sick.

Paris is the best place to be if you've got to be hopelessly in love, because of it's being so gay, as I was just saying. And Migo shut me up if I started going on too much. You can be hell's boring when you're in love. I mean you try to think it's all a big joke but you just can't. You try and think of things to make you scream with laughter but you just don't find them funny. In fact I don't think love on the whole is very jokey really.

Then old François caused a diversion. Poor old François. He was the most good-looking man you've ever seen. You know, tall, slim, bronzed, Grecian features and a medal on a piece of leather round his neck. He played the guitar in a relaxed way, giving you deep looks every now and then. I never know what to do when people give me deep looks. I usually stare out of the window and pretend I'm thinking.

I met him because I wore a hat for a bet. You wouldn't think that was very daring unless you've lived round the Left Bank. It's just one of those things you never do, wear a hat. Anyway I was dared to wear this hat in one of the students' restaurants. Boy, you try it. They drum their knives and forks on the tables until you take it off, shouting 'Chapeau' like the revolutionaries shouting 'À la guillotine'. When they all started shouting at me I pretended I didn't understand (it was a very English hat). So old François came up and explained to me in English that I had to take it off, or they'd do it for me. I refused because it was part of the bet that you had to keep it on for ten minutes. I must say I got pretty nervous when they all started to get up and move in on me. I could see my entrails scattered all over the Boul' Mich, and headlines: 'English Student torn to Bits;' 'Peer's Daughter Savaged in Restaurant.' Or only a very small paragraph at the bottom of page six: 'The arm of a woman, believed to be English, was found outside a *pissoir* in Paris last night. The French police are making inquiries.'

I didn't get savaged because old François marched me out of the restaurant, fighting off pursuers. He looked madly noble, guitar in one hand, me in the other. After that I was rather stuck with him. You can't just drop a man who has rescued you from the jaws of death, but he was so damned boring sometimes I wished I'd never won that bet. He thought he was the complete James Dean. Especially on Saturday nights; he'd get terribly droopy over his guitar and look tortured by Life, and all wrought up inside. Then on Sunday he'd be the po old Frenchman sitting in church with his mother and wearing one of those ghastly French suits.

Migo and I decided to go home for Christmas, because Christmas abroad can be pretty depressing. I mean they don't do the same thing or anything, and it could make you miserable no one doing the right things. I don't want to be corney, but that's one thing I don't like about being grown up: Christmas isn't the same. I mean it's funny and all that, and you get presents and stuff, but it's not mysterious like when you were young. Everyone spends the whole time quarrelling. Honestly our family have all their quarrels at Christmas. They save them up the whole year and then have them at Christmas. They sit about after they've eaten lunch and opened their presents (swopping the bills so they can take them back again) and quarrel about who was rude to who before the war. You should hear them. I don't know how they remember so far back, but they do.

We went back by boat, because my mother is scared stiff of aeroplanes. I'm not, I like aeroplanes, but my mother doesn't and she was paying, so we went by boat. We had tea with a whole lot of finishing-school types on the boat. They were coming home for Christmas too, and a lot of them weren't going back. None of them had learnt any French, they hadn't gone to Paris to learn French, just to get finished. I don't know how you get finished but anyway they had. Migo said it was just so that their mothers could stomp about showing off about them.

My mother was waiting on the platform when we got to Victoria. I ran up and kissed her. She held me away from her, a look of horror on her face.

'Darling,' she said, 'I wouldn't have recognized you, you're so *fat*.'

I looked down.

'Gawd, so I am,' I said.

I was too.

3

My cousin said that being fat wasn't so bad as having spots, but I didn't believe her. My mother said that she'd got fat when she'd lived in France, and my aunt told me to go and buy a girdle. I drew some money from my savings and went along to a shop in Knightsbridge. A woman with a face like a chamber-po showed me into a cubicle.

'Madam's measurements?'

I told her, but she didn't believe me. You could see that. She came back with a tape-measure. I took off my coat, and she put the tape-measure round me. She gave little low whistles as she moved down my figure, and they weren't admiration, I can tell you.

'I think Madam has altered a little since she was last measured,' she said, giving me a pussy little smile. Then she came back with a great bundle of these corset things. They were horrible. Monsters with millions of straps and suspenders everywhere. She went out and I put one on. It took some doing, I can tell you, because they had lacing everywhere. Then I looked at myself in the mirror. It was horrible. The suspenders swung round my ankles, and yards of pink cageing reached down to my knees. I turned sideways. I felt like suicide. I just thought I'd spend the rest of my life getting into pink cages. I would have jumped out of the window except that damn woman would have been so thrilled.

The awful thing about being fat is you can't get away from it. Everywhere you go, there it is, all round you: hanging and swinging, yards and yards of it, under your arms, everywhere. And everyone else is so thin. When I got out of that shop, *everyone* in Knightsbridge was thin. You've never seen so many thin people. Everyone on the bus was thin, and the girl I went to tea with looked as if she'd had mange. She tried on my belt and pulled it in five holes.

'It's a bit big for me, but then I've got a very small waist,' she said comfortingly. I hated her thin bottomless figure. Rotten thin girl. Anyway my dog made a pool on her carpet.

I got asked to a Hunt Ball after Christmas. Christmas time, as every girl worth her weight in horseflesh knows, is Hunt Ball time. The weediest weed you've ever seen asked me to one. I accepted because my mother said, you never knew who you were going to meet, and he might have friends. She always says that about weeds. Either he might have friends or he's a U.P. (Useful Person). My mother knows lots of U.P.s. She doesn't particularly like them, they're just useful.

This weed was a small long-haired thing with suède shoes. When I met him at the station he was wearing one of those Tyrolean hats with feathers and badges stuck round the band. With his horrible old chinless face underneath he made me heave, he really did. I was quite polite to him to begin with, but he went to sleep after a bit and snored with his mouth open. It was a nice day so I hummed a bit and felt quite happy.

When we arrived the other end the weed woke up, and a scarfed lady in trousers met us at the barrier. She looked quite human for a horse.

'I'm glad you managed to catch that bloody train,' she said, and while the weed was putting the suitcases in the boot she said, 'Has he been a bore?'

I nodded.

'Yes he always is,' she said, and winked. Quite jokey really.

This Horse had a very beautiful house. It was Tudor with super long drive, and smelling like an antique shop inside: lots of unclean ancestors and medieval tooth-picks on the walls, and huge cold bedrooms. We had tea in the drawing room, sitting miles apart from each other and balancing scones on our knees. The Horse talked away in a loud voice with her feet apart, and ate sandwiches in one swallow. There was another boy besides the weed, a tall fair-haired type called Michael, in an expensive suit and a watch-chain. The Ball was being held in a place called Elkerthley Castle. Pronounced Elly. It's a game all that stuff: Churpoughlin-Chulin; Smith spelt Smiffe. You can't win.

I changed jumping up and down, dressing with one hand and rubbing myself to keep warm with the other. The Horse came and fetched me to go downstairs. She was wearing horse harness, or regulation pink for lady horses at Hunt Balls: halter neck, scraggy bodice and hangy mag from the waist down. She told me a bit about who was coming.

'The Boddington Smyths, very well known in the County, some very good hunters, the Scudderburns, no stable to speak of. But quite nice. Sir Henry and Lady Piltwhistle, Jane and Miranda; and Nigel Denthead to make up the numbers.'

Michael and the weed were in the drawing room when we went in. The Horse gave us all drinks, and I talked to Michael who wasn't swoony but better than the weed any day. Weeds get frightfully possessive when they take you to dances. They go on as if you're engaged to them or something. Always looking at you or passing you peanuts and getting absolutely furious if you dance with someone else. I think they think that when they pay for your ticket they've bought you for the evening. It makes me nervous. I keep thinking everyone else is thinking I *mean* to be dancing with a weed, when I don't at all. It's just my mother's hoping he'll have some useful friends.

Sir Henry and Lady Piltwhistle arrived with Jane and Miranda. The Horse introduced everyone, Nigel Denthead was announced, and we went into dinner.

I sat between Sir Henry and Nigel Denthead.

'Do you hunt?' Sir Henry asked as he sucked at his soup.

'Occasionally,' I said, because you couldn't be too careful.

'You'll be at the meet tomorrow?'

I grunted into my spoon. I wasn't going to be unless I could help it.

'I'm following on foot, my mare's thrown a spavin.'

'Ah,' I said, but I'm not with it spavin-wise, so he turned to Mrs Boddington Smyth and started discussing spavins with her.

I listened to everyone else during the fish. Mrs Scudderburn was being enthusiastic to Mr Boddington Smyth. She had a funny face. Not the sort that would be enthusiastic to everyone.

3

And throwing her bosom all over the place as if no one else had one. Nigel Denthead was talking to Lady Piltwhistle, poor woman. If horses had their own saints she'd be Saint Piltwhistle first class. I bet when she was pregnant she knitted four bootees instead of two.

'Where do you live?' Nigel Denthead turned his great shining face towards me.

'In London.'

'Not at the weekends too?'

'Why not, I live there.'

'Interesting,' he said, 'tell me what does one *do* at the weekends in London, I've always wondered?'

I looked at him. Damn flunkey. My grandmother always says damn flunkey, especially about bank managers. I gave him what she calls a 'look'.

He didn't look flattened by my look. He just went on being shiny and eating his chicken.

I turned back to old Sir Henry. He was discussing the price of manure with Mrs Boddington Smyth. There was a man who knew which side his dung was buttered on. On the other side of the table the weed was talking to Miranda Piltwhistle and giving those chinless wuffs weeds always give. I turned back to Nigel again and asked him where *he* lived. It was that or manure.

After the coffee the girls stomped upstairs to powder their noses. I went up to Miranda Piltwhistle in the loo. She was doing her hair. She had this fuzzy fair hair and small eyes. I can't stand fuzzy hair and small eyes. One or the other but not both.

'I love your dress,' I said, 'I've always wanted a net dress.'

She put on her lipstick in the mirror.

'You should get one.'

That was the end of that conversation. I didn't care. I hated her dress, not even a horse would have been seen dead in blue net.

Elkerthley Castle stood on top of a hill. It was pouring with rain so you left your car at the bottom and there were Land-Rovers to take you up. Everyone brought wellingtons to change into before getting in the Land-Rovers. Jane Piltwhistle got left at the bottom because she couldn't find her wellingtons. Not surprising really, because I had them on.

The beginning of a Hunt Ball always follows the same routine. All the ladies troop off and leave their coats in the loo, and on coming back spend a pleasant half-hour searching (nose to wind) for the gentlemen who have hidden themselves in the bar. My luck was way out that night. I bumped straight into old Nigel Denthead. Was he pleased! He beamed at me and grasping my arm with one wet hand steered me on to the dance-floor.

Dancing with a weed is worse than talking to one. That's what hell is going to be like. It won't be torture and groaning, it'll be dancing with a weed for ever and ever. I bet the devil won't be tall and evil, I bet he'll just be a complete weed with wet hands. And when you jive with a weed he just stands throwing you about, and looking smug while you kill yourself. That's another thing about Hunt Balls. There you are in long dresses and tiaras and you're supposed to dance like a beatnik. The band plays away at all these Charlestons and things, and you dance like a fiend looking a nit with all these petticoats and things on.

I'd only been dancing with Nigel for about a quarter of an hour when Michael came up and asked me to dance. I was so grateful to get away I practically burst being charming to him. We went to look for some orange juice, then he took me down to this night-club they'd made in the dungeons. It was meant to be terribly sexy with candles and a crooner groaning away at the microphone. Actually it wasn't at all sexy. Just pitch-black, so you couldn't see if you were dancing with the right weed or not, and damn cold. I jumped up and down to begin with, but after a bit I couldn't even feel I had any legs, so I stopped. I think Michael was probably cold too actually, because we went upstairs after half an hour of that game.

The Horse had hired a private room for the evening. When we found it Nigel and the weed were getting drunk there. Not funny drunk, just boring drunk. Michael went upstairs for some more champagne, and I sat on the sofa. When he came back, he said the cabaret was about to start. Nigel stopped being drunk and straightened his white tie. This was his big moment. He was in the cabaret. He was going to do a super solo playing the bagpipes. We all followed him downstairs to the main hall.

I didn't take much interest in the cabaret until old Nigel's turn came. With a big smile to all of us he put the pipe-thing to his lips. Good old Nigel! Sweat poured off him. We waited for a wail, but not a squeak. Then like a balloon deflating he sank slowly to his knees in a dead faint, and the bagpipes with him. He was revived with a soda-siphon, and I gave him a glass of brandy to cheer him up. He was the only amusing thing that evening, he really was. The Horse was disgusted. Didn't speak to him again that night. Said he'd let the Scots down.

The rest of the evening was pretty boring. Just dancing away with one weed or another, to keep warm more than anything. Then it was bacon-and-egg time. That's the only thing that's good about Hunt Balls, the bacon and eggs at five o'clock. I suppose it's psychological really, because it means no more weeds for that evening.

Nigel and the weed had a duel on the way home – with champagne corks. They had proper seconds and everything, but neither got hurt, unfortunately. Nigel only gave the weed a small black eye, and the weed missed, so it wasn't much fun. The two Piltwhistle girls came back and had coffee. Nigel kissed Jane in the back of the car; even she didn't look too thrilled.

We didn't get to bed till about six o'clock. Then I was practically sick when I saw hunting stuff laid out in my bedroom for me. I used to be madly brave on a horse when I was about thirteen, but since I'd been going to dances I'd given up horses in favour of weeds. Less dangerous really. And a weed will at least take you to the movies, which is more than you can say for a horse. However I couldn't think of a good excuse not to hunt, so I just thought, if you've got to, you've got to, and there's nothing you can do about it, and got into bed – with my fur stole pinned round my legs.

A nice maid woke me up at nine o'clock. She was a bit surprised to see me wearing my coat and fur stole. But she agreed it was the only way to keep warm. She helped me into breeches and boots and tied my stock for me. The boots were a bit big for me, so I stuffed them with tissue paper. I don't mind telling you I was shaking up and down when I stomped into the stable yard. The first look between you and a horse is the important one. A horse can size you up in a minute.

Everyone else was mounted and ready to move off towards the meet.

'Your animal's tacked up, we'll start off slowly if you'd like to follow,' shouted the Horse.

I looked into all the boxes till I found a rather small square cob. I led it out into the yard looking it squarely in the eyes. It wouldn't stand still while I mounted so I had to hop on one leg half-way down the road before I could get the other one over. That's the trouble with being small: you always get put on small horses, and they're much more energetic.

The meet was being held at the local pub. They handed round steaming punch, and everyone looked happy except me. I chewed a piece of chocolate and did up my girths. The Horse came up.

'Shorten your reins and stick behind me, and you'll be all right,' she said, 'and if you must come off for heaven's bloody sake come off after old Denthead.'

The field moved off and I followed Mr Boddington Smyth. He was a coward, thank goodness, and went through a gate when he thought no one was looking. Then the hounds lost the scent so we sat around and munched sandwiches and talked to a few of these nutcases that follow on foot. They're potty. No honestly, I think they're really nuts, people who follow hunts on foot. They stomp all over the countryside just to see a few horses' behinds disappearing over the other side of a hedge. Then they go home quite happy. That's all they want out of life, just to see a few horses' behinds. Then they die quite happy. Some of them even do it twice a week: not only on Saturdays; they sometimes do it on Thursdays too. Just stomp, stomp, after these horses' behinds.

We moved off again, and we were going really rather well when old Boddington Smyth pulled up suddenly.

'There he is,' he shouted, 'after the bastard.'

'Who?' I asked.

'Bloody anti-blood-sports snoop. Taking filthy photographs again. Bloody Socialist. After the brute, we'll have his blood.'

He plunged his spurs into his horse's sides and I followed him.

The little anti-blood weed saw us coming and started running towards the road, his camera bouncing up and down. Then he fished a bicycle out of the hedge and peddled furiously up the road, his mac flapping in the breeze. We would have lost him if his mac hadn't caught in his wheel and practically strangled him. I thought it was jolly bad luck. I didn't think it was fair to throw his camera in the pond after that. But Boddington Smyth wouldn't listen, and he wouldn't let me help the poor thing unstrangle himself. He said he was to be left there to rot. I don't know if he's still there, I really don't. It was quite a deserted bit of country so he might be.

The Horse was thrilled when I told her. She said it was the nicest thing she'd heard for ages. Made her day. When I said it was a bit unfair to leave him to rot, she said what did I want to do, tuck him up in bed with a kiss?

4

Migo and I were quite glad to get back to Paris. Migo hadn't met a superman during the holidays. She'd collected a few new weeds but nothing much to speak of. I hadn't either actually. I went to see my old actor once in his dressing-room. Migo came with me. We took quite a long time trying to decide whether it was chasing someone to go and see them in their dressing-room, but in the end we decided it wasn't. I wanted to look frightfully *femme fatale,* so I wore a black dress and a black ribbon round my neck. The bodice of the dress was rather big for me, so I stuffed one or two of my father's socks down my bra to make me look bosomy. Sort of earth-mother appeal I thought. Migo said she thought sixteen was a bit young to develop earth-mother appeal. But I said the Italians were like that when they were sixteen. She said I wasn't Italian.

I was hell's nervous in spite of those socks to boost my bust. It was all right during the play, and in the intervals I had a few vodkas, but when it came to actually walking round I kept on thinking of why I shouldn't go. The stage-door man looked very sneery when we asked to see him.

'You needn't look like that,' I said in a sort of bored voice, 'I'm not going to rape him.' But he just went on sneering.

I couldn't bring myself to knock on his door. I kept on dashing towards the fire escape. So Migo did it for me.

He looked very sweet, this actor. He really did. With holes in his vest. I think holes in a vest can be very endearing. There was this other woman there too. I think she was in love with him too. But I wasn't jealous. I bet she loved him because he was amusing and handsome. I bet she didn't think once about him having an innocent smile. She probably didn't think he was innocent at all.

Anyway he talked more to me than he did to her. I'm not a bitch, but I couldn't help feeling triumphant because she was at least twenty-five. She kept on giving me great looks of hate, really as if she could have killed me. It was a good thing she didn't know about my father's socks, she wouldn't half have mocked me, honestly.

I made a big resolution not to think about him in Paris. It's perfectly feeble to go swooning round the place about someone who isn't there, and anyway isn't swooning over you. Besides being very boring. I did keep a small bottle of scent he gave me when he was in Paris though. It was one of those samples you get given sometimes. I asked Migo and she said it wouldn't be cheating to keep it. So I did. Every now and then I had a look at it, but mostly I was quite good.

We found Paris just the same when we got back. A bit more beautiful, because it was beginning to be summer. There were tons of bronzed Scandinavian types at the Sorbonne. Marvellously blond and healthy and shining white teeth. Funny thing though, because someone told me that if you actually go to Scandinavia none of the people who actually live there look like that. It's just a front they put up when they're abroad.

My mother said I had to learn to cook. She's keen on cooking and things as I've told you. I asked around where the best place to go was, and someone suggested a cooking-school just off the Boul' Mich. Migo and I went along and enrolled for ten lessons, every Monday and Wednesday. There were about six other girls doing it with us. Well, at least they weren't all girls. Some of them were quite old and married. There was one American woman whose husband was going to divorce her unless her cooking improved. She was very sad about it. He was in the army, stationed just outside Paris, and she said he preferred eating with the men to eating at home. She had pebble glasses and enormous feet and gym-shoes, so I don't think her cooking was the only reason.

We had to wear nylon overalls, and everyone was given a different course to cook. Migo had to make strawberry ice-cream and I had to do *pot-au-feu,* and this American woman had to do savoury tartlets. They sound pretty simple. But they're not when you've got an old French hag shouting at you. This American woman had to roll out her pastry nine times, and then when she started putting the savoury on to the pastry she was so short-sighted she made neat little piles all over the table instead of on the pastry.

Migo's strawberry ice-cream was no picnic either. She had to grind away for hours at this eighteenth-century strawberry-crushing machine. That's the thing about French cooking; they never use anything that hasn't been around for a least fifty years. And they never wash their saucepans. That's why everything has a better flavour in France. No, honestly, there's nothing like hygiene for making things tasteless. And, if they buy a Hoover, they carry on about how marvellous it is, then go back to using a broom. They're traditionalists really.

I felt quite happy about my *pot-au-feu*. It just meant cutting up millions of vegetables and chucking them into a saucepan and leaving them.

When everything had been cooked we had to sit down and eat it and discuss it. People said pretty wet things, because it's jolly difficult to think up things to say about something you've seen being dropped round the floor or scraped off a stove.

I was still feeling happy about my old *pot-au-feu* when I went downstairs to fetch it. Then I had a taste. It was fantastic. All the vegetables were absolutely raw. They'd been cooking for about three hours so you'd have thought they would have been all right. I turned the gas up and tried to boil them a bit more, and poured in tons of salt. But it didn't make any difference. I felt pretty keyed up about taking it upstairs and having everyone talking about it. I thought of dropping the dish on the stairs, but it was too much trouble. Besides, I'd have to spend hours and hours picking up every pea. The French never waste a thing.

I gave them all a big smile when I went in and said,

'I think you're really going to enjoy this.'

Then went round holding the dish while everyone helped themselves. There was a lull before they began to eat. I couldn't take it. I took the dish downstairs and paced up and down the kitchen, praying. I couldn't hear any screams of rage from upstairs. Then Migo appeared, carrying the dirty plates and screaming with laughter.

'Quick, run before she catches you,' she said, 'she's broken a tooth on one of your carrots.'

I flew, tearing off my nylon apron, with small green recipes floating from the pockets. I know I shouldn't have. It wasn't chivalrous, I should have stayed and done the decent thing. But I couldn't have afforded to pay for a Frenchwoman's tooth. Teeth are terribly expensive in France. Honestly, they cost a fortune.

We had to find another cooking-school after that. Not such a good one, but they didn't ask for *pot-au-feu*. Migo said it didn't matter about that woman's tooth because it was only a back one. I said, was she sure it was a carrot that broke it, and she swore it was. Rather funny really because you'd never think a carrot could break someone's tooth. Migo said it was probably the way I cut them up.

A huge dark-haired weed called Jeremy rang up one evening and asked me to go out with him. I'd met him at a dance during the summer. I thought he was quite nice then. He'd told me all about wanting to be a monk. I think he must have forgotten about it. I was watching at the window for him the following morning, when he came chugging into the courtyard on a motor-bike. I'd never known a man who went about on a motor-bike before. He had one of those hats and goggles and everything. He took them off and did his hair in the mirror of this motor-bike.

When he came up to fetch me, I introduced him to Madame. She thought he was swoony, because he spoke this marvellous French. It really was brilliant actually. And there's nothing the French like better than someone speaking marvellous French. I didn't listen to his French much though. I just kept looking at his head. He had frightfully smooth brown hair all plastered down, except for one bit that stuck straight up in the air like a flag at the back of his head. It kept on waving about as he talked. I don't think Madame noticed because she was swooning, but I couldn't take my eyes off it.

After a bit of chat with Madame we went off to lunch on his motor-bike. I sat side-saddle at the back, and he put his hat on again, so I couldn't see this bit of hair. But when we got to the restaurant he took it off, did his hair all over again and left the same old bit sticking up. I wondered if it was his personal aerial. I made myself stop looking at it during lunch. It's no good letting a bit of hair ruin your lunch. We talked a bit about what we were going to eat, then I said,

'That's a jolly good motor-bike you've got.'

He looked as if I'd hit him.

'That's not a motor-bike,' he said, 'it's a Vespa. Don't you know the difference between a motor-bike and a Vespa?'

I said, no I didn't, and he spent the rest of lunch drawing engines on the tablecloth. Then he trundled me off to the Champs Élysées, where he was taking part in this Rally. It was just about to start when we arrived. There were millions of Vespas all decorated with garlands of flowers, and practically every nationality in national costume sitting on them ready to go up the Champs Élysées. It was very gay, it really was. I didn't mind Jeremy's bit of hair or anything. I just chatted away with all these types. Then a super-looking Italian came up and asked me if I would sit on the back of his Vespa, because the girl he was meant to be taking felt ill.

It's very heady stuff driving up the Champs Élysées on the back of a Vespa, kissing your hand to the cheering crowds. When we reached the top I got off and a gendarme sat me on one of the traffic lights. I couldn't stop laughing. I had that fantastic feeling when you're going to burst any minute. You just feel you could pick up everything and take a bite out of it like a piece of cake. Great slices of sky, Champs Élysées, gendarme. Everything.

Jeremy was frightfully peeved because I hadn't gone on the back of his Vespa. Actually I never found out what the point of the Rally was, because we went off to tea and never rejoined the others again. I was sad because I liked that Italian. I expect he was pretty boring, but you can't tell if you don't speak Italian. Even 'pass the butter' is exciting if you can't understand what they're saying. I went on going out with Jeremy after that. But after a bit I really couldn't stand it. I mean it wasn't only engines the first couple of times, he was really interested in them. He really liked the way engines worked and how fast they went and everything. Madame was frightfully disappointed when I stopped going out with him. Mostly because he kissed her hand, and spoke this wonderful French. I tried to explain about the engines, but she didn't understand. He didn't talk to her about engines.

Of course the French absolutely hate the English. They just pretend to be swoony about them so they can spend their summer holidays in England. And once they are in England, they're a dead bore. No really. There's nothing you can show them they haven't got better in old France. And they spend the whole time writing air-mail letters and reading piles of French magazines. Then when they go back to France they carry on for ever about how '*sensationnel*' everything in England is. And pretend they had fantastic romances with men the dead spit of the Duke of Edinburgh.

Madame had a huge fat char called Madame Geneviève who loathed the English. Ever since she spent a month in Eastbourne when she was seventeen. She said she'd never recovered. She used to lie in wait for me every morning pretending to wash up while I ate my breakfast. She always said the same thing to begin with:

'*Quand j'étais à Eeeeestbourne . . .*'

Then we'd be off. Every morning we went from *croissants* to Agincourt. She said everyone knew that the only good thing in England was *le cardigan anglais* and *le duc d'Édinbourg*. Honestly. She couldn't even admit that English loos were better than French ones. She said they were just different. She said, '*La coutume est différente, c'est tout.*' I'll say.

As the weather got hotter Migo went on a lot of these coach trips to stately homes that her club organized. She loves clubs and evening classes and all that. Honestly, she'll join anything. I once went to a keep-fit class with her. It was terrifying: huge women with fantastic muscles skipping about in swim-suits doing dainty gym, swinging clubs and skipping ropes and pointing their toes all over the place. I nearly died I was so embarrassed. Migo loved every minute, she said it did her good psychologically. She came out feeling a new and better person.

She took me on one of these stately-home coach trips once. I went with her and this other friend of hers called Birgitte Applestrohm. She was quite a girl old Birgitte. Very sexy. You could see she was. Even if you were a girl. I mean, often men swoon and you just can't see what they're swooning about, but you could with Birgitte. Migo said that she had great hordes of clean American lovers. Very clean and white-toothed with big chests, Migo said they were. She brought one of these types with her on this coach trip.

We started off early with a picnic lunch, and I wore a straw hat. This American kept on pushing it on to my nose. He thought he was being really funny. He didn't only do it once. He kept on doing it, and then splitting his sides. I got a bit fed up I can tell you. Then Migo and I were munching away at our sandwiches during lunch and he came gambolling up with Birgitte and practically sat on top of us, under this tree. It gave Migo indigestion them being under this tree.

'They think they're the latest thing from Zola, full of milky bosom and hidden desire,' she said to me. 'Elma's giving her sun-kissed embraces.'

'You're just jealous,' I said.

'Oh yes, I'm green,' said Migo, 'I can't wait to lie laughing in the arms of a blond beast with a crew-cut, capped teeth and a bag of contraceptives in his pockets.'

We walked round the gardens after that because Migo was getting a bit cross. I knew what she meant actually. Frightfully clean people make me feel much sicker than any other sort of person. They're not like people at all; they're like vegetables wrapped in Cellophane. They don't look like vegetables at all. I once went to stay with some people whose daughter married a friend of my cousin. I just happened to be there when they got back from their honeymoon. They were both bronzed and very beautiful, and her mother kept on purring on about how marvellous they looked together. And how ecstatic they were and all that. But do you know every time I looked at them, I'm not joking, I felt really ill. Honestly, physically sick. They were so beautiful they didn't care about anyone. Not even each other. They were the sort of people old Hitler would have swooned over.

If you want to know about old Birgitte, she had to marry that drip. Migo said she didn't want to, she just thought she ought to. Pretty depressing having to marry someone because you're pregnant. Poor dear I bet she got to regret those easy sunny kisses.

I don't think I'll ever have to marry anyone actually. 'Course you can't be absolutely certain about anything, but I don't think I will. My family don't tend towards sex really. I don't think I do either. I mean I find it frightfully difficult to take sex seriously. No honestly. I think it's terribly difficult to take sex seriously if you've got a sense of humour. If you think of any sex maniacs you know, they haven't got a real sense of humour. They've got a sense of fun all right, but not a real sense of humour. The Tendency in my family is drink. My brother hasn't got it: I have but he hasn't. When I was at school I kept vodka in my tooth mug. And once at a house feast I got pickled on cider because I drank all the prefects', and no one was ever allowed to have it again. They had to put me to bed singing 'God Bless the Pope'.

It's not funny having this Tendency actually. The worst I ever got drunk was when my brother came to see me in Paris. He turned up one evening with a very relaxed friend. He was the most relaxed man you've ever met. He was so relaxed at Cambridge he got sent down. Anyway they were feeling very extravagant because they were only in Paris for the weekend, so we rang up a French bird and arranged to meet her at a cinema in the Champs Élysées. She was very pretty this girl. And very smart. The boys brightened up like mad, and I did too. No, really I did. I like pretty girls, they're much easier to get on with than ugly ones. I suppose it's because they usually have a better time.

The movie we went to see was very sad and beautiful. It was the sort of movie that makes you feel lonely inside. Like when you're in love. You feel all gone inside and empty. That's when you get this Tendency, because you just make for a bottle to make you stop thinking about this all gone inside feeling. Anyway I had this feeling from seeing this movie so when we got to the restaurant I started to drink. It was the perfect place, because there were Russian fiddlers and everyone else was pretty tiddly and singing and laughing. It was the sort of place you want to dance a wild fandango before you've been there a minute. We had a few vodkas to begin with, and toasted the Czar. It was splendid except for the French girl.

She wouldn't drink a thing. She sat looking very po saying she'd just have a lemonade. My brother's friend thought she was sweet. I didn't. I thought she was a drip. I can't bear people who won't be super and wild when you should be. I started talking to everyone and singing. 'Course the more po this girl looked the more wild I got. You know how you do, if someone disapproves. Luckily the boys joined in, so she faded away into a corner until we were very very tiddly indeed. When we got out of the restaurant she went home by herself in a taxi, and we tried to think where we'd left the car. But this relaxed boy kept on saying to my brother,

'Your sister looks just like Gertrude Lawrence.'

And we'd all stop thinking about the car and scream with laughter. In the end we got a taxi and went to look for the car. We couldn't find it, so we went to the boys' hotel instead. They went upstairs to get something, and I sat in the hall and waited for them. There was an old woman trying to persuade the man behind the desk to let her take a boy with her upstairs. I think she was going to seduce him. Anyhow the man wouldn't let her. I didn't blame him. She was screaming drunk and foul. I went to the mirror and did my hair. Suddenly I looked from her face to mine. It was awful. Honestly I looked as beastly as she did. Drunk and disgusting. I thought, I'll end up like her. It starts off like this. You get drunk because you feel all gone inside, then you end up like her. Probably worse. Lying in a gutter somewhere with people spitting on you. I've never been tiddly like that again. I've often wanted to be, but I haven't. Tendencies are no joke.

I'll tell you another thing that gives me that all gone feeling. Strauss waltzes. You know, when I dance one of those waltzes I think I'm going to die. Only I don't, I go on living, and that's much worse. My last evening in Paris I danced one of those waltzes with the Count. Then we walked round Paris for hours and hours. Pretty corney I suppose. But I wanted to remember Paris exactly as it was then. Then, when I was seventeen. So that when I'm eighty and crippled with age and disillusioned and bitter, I'll have Paris to look at as if I'm seventeen. Disillusion and bitterness won't matter. I'll have one huge beautiful thing to look at without sadness. I've often wondered if you could do that with a person. Just remember them as they are when you love them most, and keep that in front of you and never notice when they're ghastly. 'Course there's always the risk I won't get embittered. But it wasn't a risk I could take with Paris.

I stood and watched the dawn break over Paris from the Sacré Cœur. Even the Count shut up. It was unimaginable. Cold and silent. And the sky like – I don't know – heaven, I suppose. And corney old Paris.

5

When I got back to London, my mother said I had to do a secretarial course. I wasn't too pleased about that I can tell you. I said I didn't want to do a secretarial course. And she said, well, what did I want to do? I said I wanted to be 'discovered'. She said, doing *what*? So I did a secretarial course.

My real trouble is I'm absolutely normal, and I've got no ambition. Don't think I feel all right about being normal, because I promise you I don't. I don't go about being smug about it, honestly. It's not just *now* I'm normal. I mean I haven't just begun to be normal. I've been completely normal my whole life. Honestly, ever since I was born.

I suppose it began when I was born. First of all I was completely healthy. I wasn't purple, and no one was worried about whether I was going to live or anything, and my mother didn't hate me. It would have been all right being healthy if my parents hadn't wanted me, but they had. That was a bad start. Then when I got a bit older I was good tempered and had a good appetite, and did perfectly normal things like running away from school. It's been a great burden to me. Being normal. And I've never had a neurosis, no really, not one. And no complexes either. So that's why I submitted to doing a secretarial course. And if you want the truth, that's the worst thing about doing a secretarial course. Having to be normal. And going round with everyone else who is being normal and doing a secretarial course too. It worried me no end, going round with these normal people. But I didn't do anything about it to begin with.

My mother knew about me being in love with this actor, but she didn't do anything about it until one evening when we were alone. Then she began to ask me what happened in Paris. I didn't know what to say. When people talk about things they seem to distort them. Everything gets boiled down to motives or generalized. You just feel an enormous cliché: the eternal young innocent in love with the older man. And it's not that at all. You know you're the old, old story, but that's not it. You're not really innocent, he's not really old. It's just that he's perfect.

Anyway, after she'd hedged about a bit, I said,

'Oh well, I suppose I'm in love with him, but it doesn't matter, I'll get over it.'

She gave me a worried look.

'Don't you think it would be a good idea to try to forget him?'

'Why?' I said.

'I could tell you why, but I don't want you to be disillusioned.'

'It's all right, I don't mind being disillusioned. I don't *like* being in love.' She paused then she said,

'He's going to marry that girl he's acting with at the moment. She saw him off at the airport when he came to Paris, didn't he tell you?'

Then suddenly I could hear time rushing by me. Honestly it sounds stupid, but I could hear myself talking and watch myself. You know like when you're drunk sometimes.

'You mustn't be hurt, darling,' she said, 'men love young girls because they're innocent and flattering.'

'Oh,' I said, 'I didn't expect him to take me seriously. I just loved him. Stupid really.'

I didn't cry, I just went to bed. I didn't mind about him going to marry that actress, I just minded about her seeing him off at the airport. Honestly that was the only thing I minded about. It just made when he was in Paris seem like nothing. It probably was nothing to him. He was probably yawning his head off. But I remembered that I'd rushed into his arms and laughed and shouted and practically broke his hand holding on to it. I couldn't believe it was him, for heaven's sake. He probably gave that pottery thing we bought in Montmartre to his old actress. God, you feel a fool when you think about things like that, because you really think they're perfect. Just nothing wrong with them.

I believed her though. My mother, I mean. But I still had to go and see for myself. I was pretty nervous because I always was when he was about. His flat was at the top of a long staircase, so when the maid let me in all I could do was pant. The room was full of sunlight, and he was in bed with 'flu, or something and there was another man there. I stood looking at them panting and shading my eyes. He said hello and introduced me to the man. I sat on his bed and talked to them for a bit, and this other man kept on asking him how he was every five minutes. He had a photograph of his old actress on the wall. She looked quite pretty. I didn't mind. I just minded about him probably having given her that pottery face.

I looked at him when he was talking to the other man, and he wasn't perfect any more. Just a man in bed with 'flu. The other man went, and he said,

'Can you see my cigarettes?' I had a look round and couldn't, then he said,

'I think they're under the bed.'

So I bent to pick them up and my knees cracked. They always do, I used to lose five marks every ballet exam. Anyway he pretended not to notice when my knees cracked, and I gave him the cigarettes and said,

'I think I'd better go. I'm meant to be at a lunch party.'

And he said,

'I'll ring you up and ask you to a movie one evening.'

And I said,

'Yes, that'd be super.'

And I walked out into Mayfair feeling rather relieved actually. He wasn't perfect any more. I wasn't in love any more. I suddenly realized I wouldn't have to be nervous or feel like hell any more. Not ever again. Then I thought: What am I going to *think* about? What was I going to wish for? I couldn't think of a thing.

Perhaps you don't understand, but you've got to wish for something the whole time when you're seventeen. You've got to, or there's nothing to live for. However impossible you've got to *think* you want it. It doesn't matter if it's a superman or a sports car, it's got to be something. Or you want to commit suicide. When I couldn't think of a thing I wanted I nearly did. I nearly stepped in front of a bus in Notting Hill Gate. I just happened to see a rather cheery dog on the other side of the road, so I didn't.

What with not having anything to think about and doing a secretarial course with all these normal people I was pretty depressed, I can tell you. But when you're depressed I think you should start again. You know. Do corney things like changing your hairstyle, and getting a new lot of weeds. So I changed my hair. I had this enormous beehive. Well, the girl in the shop said it was a beehive, but my father said it was a bird's nest, and I looked better before I went in. He said why pay good money to some old hairdresser, he could do the same thing free. He can be quite boring like that. I mean he thinks he's being pretty funny, and my mother thinks he is too. I think he's a bit feeble really. When he goes on like that, I mean. Most of the time he's all right.

When I'd changed my hairstyle and got a few new weeds, I still didn't feel very jokey. So I thought, hell, I'll have a go at being a beatnik. I knew it wouldn't be easy because of being so normal. Also I didn't know any beatniks. I just knew girls who were going to be debs, and they were no use. I didn't look much like a beatnik either, in spite of the beehive. But then I thought I'd be dead cunning. I'd look so like a real beatnik that no one would find out that I was really normal. I knew if they found out I was normal I'd had it.

So okay I'd got a beehive. Now I wanted a jumper. You only need one jumper if you're a beatnik. If you change your jumper you lose your identity. I asked Migo about this jumper. She had a cousin who'd been a beatnik. Or had a boy friend who'd been one or something. Anyway she found one of her father's gardening jumpers that he'd been through the First World War in. It had a few bullet-holes, so you could tell it was genuine all right. It was very long. Down to my knees. And it had a collar you could pull over your face if you didn't want to see anyone. With my tight jeans and beach shoes, I looked the real thing I really did.

There was a pretty drippy beatnik in my class at secretarial college. I stood her a coffee and a cheese-cake a couple of times, so she'd help me join the Chelsea Set. It was worth it, because she arranged to take me to a Saturday-night party with a couple of male beatniks. She was really wet this girl, but you can't pick and choose your beatniks if you only know one. She was a bit doubtful about whether I'd be all right, because I looked so normal at college. However, I spun her a great story about my mother hating me, and having to live at home because I'd no money.

She lived in a flat with three other beatniks. She said she was looking for a man to live with. So far she'd had no luck. I'm not surprised actually, because she really was wet. I said, why didn't she live with a beatnik? She said it was too expensive. She couldn't afford it. They ate such a lot. And besides she didn't know any that were house-trained.

I was a bit nervous when I turned up at her flat for this Saturday-night party she'd asked me to, in case she'd tell me I looked too normal to come. I pulled my jumper up to cover my nose, so only my eye make-up could be seen, and rang the bell. I'd been practising this hop up and down that I knew beatniks did, and I started to do it when she opened the door. Then I sort of slid sideways up the hall corridor. She looked quite approving so I think I was quite good at it.

These two male beatniks were in the drawing-room when we went in. They were sitting on the floor. At least one was sitting on the floor, and the other was behind one of the armchairs. Me and this girl sat on the floor too. Then she introduced me to the one sitting on the floor near us. He was called Webb and he wore these monk's sandals. I don't think he washed his feet. It didn't look as if he did anyway. He didn't talk much either, just sort of grunted. I don't think he was in a talking mood. After a bit we crawled round to talk to the other one behind the armchair. He was called Spence. He wore these really corney gold-rimmed glasses. He was much worse than Webb. And he was frightfully sweaty. I mean his shirt really stuck to him. I don't swoon over men who sweat a lot, I really don't. Nor does my mother. She's always thanking God my father doesn't sweat. She says she doesn't know what she'd do if he did. You know, some men have only got to start talking to you and they start sweating. And taking out their hankies and mopping themselves every two minutes. This beatnik Spence, he was that type. Really sweaty.

After we'd talked to Spence for a bit, we thought we'd go to this party. It wasn't very far. Just round the corner from this girl's flat, so we walked. It was terribly windy, which was maddening, because by the time we arrived I looked really healthy. Honestly, blooming and rosy. I nearly killed myself, because I'd spent hours putting on this green powder I'd bought. I mean, except for being normal, looking healthy is the worst thing that can happen to a beatnik. Even if you're abnormal as hell and shaking with neurosis, if you look healthy no one's going to believe you. Luckily I'd bought some dark glasses so I put them on and they covered most of my face up and my jumper covered the other half of it. So no one could really make sure that I was healthy.

The party was in the garage of one of those small mews houses. You know the kind. It was pretty crowded by the time we arrived. I mean, people were beginning to stand on each other and things. They don't usually start standing on each other till it gets crowded. Not usually. I crouched by the wall, while Spence went and got me a drink. That's the first principle about being a beatnik: if you don't know anyone you mustn't let on. I mean you mustn't *look* as if you don't know anyone. If you're alone you must look as if you're thinking, or brooding about your mother, or something. Don't for heaven's sake look as if you'd like to talk to someone. Talking to someone, I mean sort of chit-chat about this and that, is strictly for the birds. So I crouched by the wall as I was saying, till Spence came back with the drink. I sunk my head right down, and twisted my legs in a faintly Yogi-type way. A little bit of Yoga or Zen Buddhism is very useful. I'd seen a programme on television about Yogis so I knew a bit about it.

When Spence rolled up with a bottle of wine I pretended not to notice him. It's quite a good thing not to notice people. Anyway I pretended not to notice him, so he began to scratch. Honestly, I don't know what his chest was like but he made a noise like a nutmeg-grater. Backwards and forwards, louder and louder, so in the end I raised my head and looked at him. He went on scratching with one hand and handed me the bottle of wine with the other. I gave him a sinister look through my dark glasses and took the bottle and drank. He took it back and had a swig himself. Then he said,

'Man.'

That really bored me. Him saying that. For heaven's sake, talk about type casting. There is a limit. I stood up and leant against the wall and groaned. I've got a good groan, so Spence looked quite taken with me standing and groaning. Then he said,

'Let's roll.'

But I pretended not to hear and just went on groaning, so he took my hand and dragged me towards the other end of the garage where people were dancing. I really felt like groaning then. I told you he was sweaty; well, you can imagine it was no picnic dancing with him. He clutched me to his damp shirt and danced slowly up and down breathing heavily with steam rising from him. In fact he never made much progress because he kept on stopping, and having to take his glasses off and wipe the steam from them.

Then a girl started screaming. You wouldn't have heard unless you were near like we were. They were really agonizing screams.

'What's with her screaming?' I said.

'Her father's a duke,' Spence said.

She was in a real state this girl, sobbing and shouting that her life was ruined and things. My father's a corney old lord but I don't let it ruin my life. I mean you've had it if you let things like that get you down.

'Let's go upstairs,' I said.

Spence scratched himself for a bit then agreed. So we crawled across the garage and up the stairs to the kitchen. There were a whole lot of bodies necking on the landing carpet, so it took a bit of getting into the kitchen. There was someone sitting in the sink reading a book and eating cheese. Quite a nice face I thought, but I didn't say anything. I put a string of onions round my neck and lay on the floor. Spence lay on the kitchen table and ate a pear. Then someone came in and said,

'Any of you booked for the bedroom?'

Spence sat up and gazed down at me on the floor.

'You booked?'

I didn't know what he meant, but I said yes, because he made me feel ill.

It turned out that the man who owned the house lent his

bedroom, and you paid a quid to go in there with some type for half an hour. This really wet beatnik girl went in there about five times. I know I'm narrow-minded but honestly you might as well be a tart. I mean, for heaven's sake, tarts get paid. She even went in there with old Webb and his monk's sandals. Still I suppose I can't judge. But Webb. Honestly you should have *seen* his feet. Old Spence was a bit fed up with me so after he'd scratched for a few minutes he slid out of the room looking furious. I didn't take any notice. I just stared up at the ceiling.

When he'd gone the man in the sink said,

'Have some cheese.'

It was good cheese so I said, 'This cheese is really mean,' in a groany kind of voice.

He agreed, and we went on like that for a bit. I got better as the evening wore on.

He was really a good beatnik, that man. He was called Herb. And he knew about things. I mean he could read and everything. And he was quite conversational. He talked to you and asked you what you thought about things. Which is very unusual. We talked for a long time actually. He sat in the sink most of the time, and I sat on the draining-board. One thing he said. He said that when you died there were probably only about five people who were strictly really sorry. He said you'd be lucky if there were five. I think he meant other than your relations. He didn't have any relations. Relations usually mind if you die because it means one less relation. It makes them feel better if they've got a lot of relations, even if they don't particularly like them.

After we'd talked about who would be sorry if we died he asked me to dance. I said okay and we went down to the garage. I tried to think about who'd be sorry on the way down to the garage. I mean I started counting them up. I know a lot of people, but I won't tell you how many'd be sorry. They'd all go to my funeral okay, but they wouldn't be sorry.

Herb was a good dancer. I was enjoying dancing with him when old Webb appeared. He flipped towards us in his old monk's sandals. He had a frightfully smug look on his face. Smug and bloated.

'That bedroom is the most,' he said. He was really corney and his face made me ill. He looked like someone who has had a really good meal, then tilts his chair with a grunt and looks pleased with himself. You know what I mean. I'd kill myself if someone looked like that after they'd slept with me. I really would. I've never slept with anyone. So I can't talk. But a lot of people talk about sex to you. I mean quite old people who are married and things, and some of them make me feel very queasy. I don't think they can have loved anyone if they talk like that.

Herb had a blank face. Not much expression or anything, but I don't think he liked old Webb either because he started dancing again while Webb was still talking. Then I trod on Webb by mistake. So I turned round and said, 'Like I hope your Webb foot's all right,' and screamed with laughter. I thought it was a pretty funny joke. Actually I always think my jokes are funny, I'm about the only person I know who laughs when they tell a joke. Really, everyone else keeps a straight face. I don't know when they're making a joke so I spend the time laughing like a maniac in case they get offended. Webb didn't think that joke was funny, so he walked off. Herb did though. You could tell he did, in spite of his having this blank face. He didn't laugh or anything. But you could tell. You don't find many beatniks who laugh actually. They scream and groan and sometimes one or two will make a joke, but it's not often you see them laugh.

We'd just started dancing again when old Spence steamed up. He was really sweating. I mean it was dripping off him.

'Someone's pinched my overcoat,' he said, and he was shaking up and down. All that beat stuff went west once he lost his overcoat. He was absolutely normal. It just shows you. Anyway Herb went off to look for it with him, and I went and asked a girl who was kissing someone by the door if anyone had left. She had these marvellous leather boots on with fur round the top. When I asked her she stopped kissing this weed and said, 'Balls.' So I said,

'Where did you buy your boots?' and she told me. She said they weren't very expensive.

It turned out that the only person who'd gone off in a black overcoat was someone in monk's sandals. Good old Webb hitting back at Society again. Spence wasn't surprised. He said

Webb had been locked in a cupboard when he was four. His subconscious never recovered. If you ask me he was probably cold.

Herb took me home about six o'clock. I got a fright when I did get in actually. My father was waiting for me. He was green. No kidding. Really green. I mean the colour of trees and leaves and things. He thought I'd been murdered or something boring. He was even more furious because I *hadn't* been murdered. Honestly, it takes a lot to make him happy. Anyway he was so furious, luckily he couldn't speak. It's much worse when he can speak. He gets frightfully witty-witty. That's much worse. Honestly much.

I went to a lot of parties after that. I didn't have to go with that wet girl because of Herb. I got to know most of the beats round Chelsea. Not all of them but most. I couldn't have stuck them if I'd had to go with that girl every time. As it was I had to go on having coffee with her at college. She was so boring. She just went on and on about how many men she'd slept with. I think she was a nymphomaniac. I don't know how you qualify, but I think she was. She was damn boring anyway. I haven't met many, but they usually are. Herb was practically the only person worth talking to at those parties. He was beat all right but he was worth talking to.

Then he got run over. I never found out how it happened. I just noticed he wasn't there. I asked someone after a couple of weeks, and they said he'd been run over. It gave me a bit of a shock actually. No one knew if he'd got buried or anything. He didn't know anyone but beats so he probably got put any old where. You wouldn't catch a beat paying for a funeral. No one minded except me. They didn't even pretend to be sad. That girl at college said, why should she be sad, she hadn't slept with him? I didn't have coffee with her after that. In fact I don't think I spoke to her again. I was sorry I stood her that cheese-cake.

I gave up being a beatnik after Herb got run over. I wasn't in love with him. Nothing like that. He was just nice. Very simple. And I liked talking to him. Beatniks were too conventional anyway. I mean they thought they were getting away from it, which is pretty corney. You never do. You just change one thing for another. I was too fat to make a good beatnik anyway. You have to be thin. No really. You've got to look T.B. or it's no good. Not only your face: all over. Still it was quite interesting.

6

After I'd been a beatnik I thought I'd have a real change. So I became a deb. I don't know why I became one actually, because I always swore I wouldn't. But you know how you become things, you sort of drift into them. No one really says anything; you just suddenly find yourself doing them.

I started off with one advantage, because of my father being a lord. If you're a deb you've got to be rich or have a title. One or the other. Of course, if you've got both, you're in clover. You can't fail. If you've neither, you might get about a bit. But nothing much to speak of. My mother was quite keen on me being a deb, because she thought it would help me forget that old actor. My father didn't say much. He never does. Except 'How much will it cost?' My brother was keen too because it meant a lot of free parties. People ask him out a lot because they've got this idea he's eligible. No honestly, they really think he's eligible because of him going to be a lord when you-know-who dies.

Actually I don't think I've told you about my brother. He's the only one I've got. I haven't got any sisters, just my cousin who's as good as. I'll tell you something about my brother. Everyone says he knows where he's going, he's got his head on the right way, and all that. But at heart he's a beatnik. He doesn't look like one because of being in the cavalry, but he is. One day he's going to stun everyone and elope with a jazz singer of forty. I hope he does. I would if I was him. He doesn't say much. He's like my father: not a great talker. But I should think he gets fed up with people saying that all the time. Mind you, I don't *know*, but I should think so. I would. Drive me barmy. Mind you, people once they start thinking one thing about you, they never stop. If they say you're just like a great-aunt, they'll go on saying you're like this great-aunt till you're a hundred. It doesn't matter if you change and become completely different, they still go on saying it.

To begin with when I started being a deb we were a bit in dickie's meadow, because my mother's not a flitty Society type. So she didn't really know any debs or their mothers. But I knew one or two girls from school who were doing the season, and some from college. So they soon mounted up. The tea parties I mean. That's how it works. You get asked to someone's tea party and meet all these girls. They take down your name and address and ask you to their tea party, and you do the same to them and ask them to yours. You scratch my back and I'll scratch yours. It's quite a good system really. A lot of mothers won't let their daughters go to someone's tea if they don't know them. But that's pretty drippy really, because knowing people's got nothing to do with it. It might have been in their day, but not any more.

Your mother is a very important bit of being a deb. She has to go to all these lunch parties and chat to other mothers. My mother found luncheon chit-chat an awful strain. She's very intelligent so that kind of conversation got her down. I used to cheer her up beforehand, and she borrowed my grandmother's diamonds and things. But it was still hard work. She was quite amusing about them afterwards though. She said the frightfully rich ones kept their minks on all through lunch. She said they'd rather melt than take them off. And everyone cheered up when they heard I had a brother. The point of being a deb is to get married I suppose, though not many of them do. But that's the object really. So a brother is good news.

Of course doing the season is expensive. It was expensive even for me and I did it on the cheap. I had all my clothes made and bought remnants. We had a jolly funny time actually. You can't help giggling when you go round buying things with 'shop soiled' on them when everyone else is flying to Paris to buy theirs. It was things like tea parties and stockings that cost the most. It was all right if the tea party was near the secretarial college or your house, but if it was miles it cost a fortune. Migo and I used to take the underground and then get a taxi and arrive looking frightfully respectable. It wasn't so easy going back, but sometimes we'd get a lift. Stockings and shoes were pretty boring though. The thing to do was to put your ladder on the inside of your leg and stick your shoes with Sellotape. It had to be expensive Sellotape because the cheap stuff doesn't last.

Most of the girls were pretty rich. Or if they weren't rich they had godmothers who left them money to do the season with. Or their parents were separated. If your parents are separated you usually have a pretty good time of it because if they marry again it's practically always someone rolling, and even if they don't they spend the time competing with each other giving you presents. Anyway even if these girls didn't notice the ladders or the Sellotape, you thought they did. You'd chat away to them and hope for the best, but they'd be quite unmoved by jokes or anything. Just stare through you. It's quite daunting having someone stare through you if your shoes are stuck with Sellotape. Most of the time I think they didn't notice actually, I think they were just rather dumb and couldn't think of anything to say.

Even if you had new shoes, tea parties were pretty sinister. You spent the whole time sitting on the floor eating sandwiches and swopping addresses. Most of the girls were nice-looking. I mean *looking* at them was okay. It was just talking to them that was awful. They spent the whole time asking you if you were going somewhere. And if you weren't they'd stop talking to you. If Janey-Lulu hadn't asked you to her luncheon you'd had it. I'm not joking. They wouldn't talk to you for days. If you mentioned anything else they thought you were potty. No really. Nuts. You couldn't blame them really, they didn't know any better. They didn't even know how to begin to talk about anything else. Nor did their mothers. It wasn't their fault.

Tea parties went on for practically ever. Everyone went on and on giving them. If they liked you they didn't only ask you to one, they asked you to about half a dozen. And if there was some corney bit in the newspapers about you they'd all swoon.

Even girls who you knew hated you. There was this girl at college like that. She really loathed me. I couldn't stand her. Do you know she hated me so much she wouldn't even let me cheat in a shorthand test. Nobody gets through shorthand without cheating. It's never been known. Anyway when she sat next to me during one of these tests she made me put the book away.

Everyone else had theirs out. But no she didn't, so I had to put mine away. Then when there was a piece in some newspaper with my face on it she practically killed herself being nice to me. She really thought I'd fall for that. For heaven's sake.

Most people give cocktail parties after they've given a whole lot of teas and lunches. Cocktail parties are worse than tea parties. They're worse than dances too, come to think of it. In fact they're the worst thing you could possibly do. Except shorthand. It's all the weeds you have to talk to. They're much worse than the girls. Millions of times worse. If you find the girls chilling you wait and see what you'll find the men. You really get fond of the girls after you've met the men. I thought I knew how weedy a weed could get. But I didn't. I didn't know even half how weedy a weed could get.

When you start going to these cocktail parties the first mistake you make is to think they want to talk to you. So you go up and start talking. You know, chit-chat about things. If a weed thinks you look all right he'll talk a bit. Then he'll start asking you where you live and how many houses you've got and whether you're giving a dance. If you've only got one house you're lucky if he stays two minutes. They don't believe in wasting time, weeds. Gosh no. They're off like a streak of lightning. I don't blame them. I don't really. If you only want to know heiresses and stuff it's no good talking to people like Migo and me. It's a simple outlook really.

You develop a technique after a bit. Cocktail party technique. First of all you don't care. Then when you go in and see rows and rows of enemy backs facing you with no gaps to break through, you don't just stand and hope. You dive through their legs and start talking non-stop at whatever you come up face to face with. You talk so fast they don't have time to ask you how many houses you've got. And you *will* them not to walk away. You've got to will jolly hard. Sometimes it doesn't work and they walk off. But you just spring on someone else, and if they walk away too you take a taxi to the next cocktail party. And start all over again.

Of course you meet the same weeds at dances, but it's not nearly so bad. Because they have to talk to you at dinner. And when you get to the dance you don't have to talk to them because you're dancing and you can pretend to be concentrating. It's a funny thing about debby weeds actually. None of them is rich or eligible or anything. In fact most of them are absolutely broke, and not a title between them. You'd think they would be because of all these heiresses swooning over them. But they're not. One man I knew quite well was a complete rotter. He didn't pretend not to be. I mean he told you that he was, which I think is quite fair. These girls' mothers paid him to take their daughters out to dinner. He said it brought in quite a steady income. And he never had to pay for anything. Tax-free too. Which isn't to be sneezed at. He had this double-barrelled name he'd made up, and he used to tell them he'd made it up and no one believed him. They thought he was joking. There's a book printed for these debby weeds listing all the girls coming out and their hobbies and how much of everything they've got. So really it's a pretty good sideline. And dead simple. You've only got to have a dinner jacket, reference books and a tennis racket for weekends and you're in business.

Loos are very important during the season. I should think they're practically the most important bit of the season for some girls. I know one girl who did her whole season in the loo. She used to take this small edition of *War and Peace* about with her in her evening bag. She got through it seven times in one season. She was quite a slow reader. Migo had a copy of *Gone with the Wind* she hid in the Dorchester loo. There were a terrible lot of dances at the Dorchester, so she just curled up with it till it was time to go home. They couldn't go home straight after dinner because their mothers would be furious and say they were failures. It's one thing to be a failure. But it's a hell if your mother keeps telling you. And some of them could go on for hours.

My brother was quite keen on all these parties to begin with. But he soon got bored. Pretty soon I can tell you. He's quite intelligent. Very intelligent actually, so debs rather got him down after a bit, after the novelty wore off. He found it was impossible to remember their names, because they were so long. And he said, even when he did remember their names, they all looked the same. So he gave up going after a bit. Except if it was a relation or something.

Country dances could be fun though. Honestly, get a weed among green foliage and pastures, and he wasn't nearly so bad. Some of them even became quite human. Made jokes and things. You usually stay the weekend with someone for dances in the country. The people who give the dance fix you up with someone who lives near. You really had a nice time if the people you were staying with were fun. It didn't even matter if the dance was bad, you could still enjoy yourself, because you had all these trees and things to look at. Even if you were bored you could enjoy the view.

It was nerve-racking if you got taken to the dance alone in a car, especially if it was a long drive. The thing is you nearly always got told who you were going with and there was nothing you could do about it. You can't tell some po old hostess you don't want to go with someone because he's a sex maniac, and being raped by a weed would be no joke. I'm not exaggerating: some of those weeds there was nothing they wouldn't stop at. Mostly because they're so stupid. No intelligence at all. So they get bored. They really live with boredom all the time. That's the reason they're so nasty most of them. They're just so bored. Nothing to think about or anything. Just dance after dance. Anyone would get nasty being bored all the time. Honestly, even a saint.

My mother used to get very cross. About these types asking if they could rape you all the time. She said they didn't go on like that in her day. She said they always brought you chocolates and flowers and you went to football matches, but they didn't rape you. I don't think she knew the same types actually. I mean, the summit of her season was the Cuckfield Hockey Dance. She was a simple country girl. I asked her what I should do about these rapey sort of weeds. She couldn't decide whether I should learn driving or have a police whistle. In the end she settled for a pepper-pot. She made me keep this pepper-pot in my evening bag. So if a weed really leaped on me with a low growl all I had to do was open my evening bag, get out the pepper-pot, unscrew the lid and chuck the pepper in his eyes, in one easy

5

movement. Migo and I practised once and it was impossible. It would be all right if you knew when they were going to leap. Then you could start undoing your bag and unscrewing the pot beforehand. But you don't. And when it was damp weather you couldn't even unscrew the top because it got all clogged up. You were really in dickie's meadow.

It wasn't only the weeds that could be nerve-racking. Some of these snobby old girls were pretty frightening. I mean girls' mothers and things. The thing is, in theory you think, pooh I'm not frightened of some old bag. But it's no good pretending because no matter what you do you still feel jolly nervous. I used to try anything. All the old gimmicks, like imagining them with nothing on and all that, but it didn't help much. You weren't always frightened of them because they were frightening, or you felt shy, or knew they were going to ask you something ghastly. Often they just frightened you because they were so horrible. Not frightening horrible. Just horrible. I'd never met people so heartless. Mind you, I hadn't met a lot of people. Though even now those smug women give me the creeps, and I'm getting on. No chicken.

I had a dance of course. And a cocktail party and everything. Rather good. I thought so anyway. I don't think my father was swoony though. Most of the time he talked to the maid downstairs. Drips and stuff aren't really his line. He'd rather be in the kitchen with a bottle of whisky. When I said why didn't he have a go at talking to some of them, he just said,

'I'm damned if I want a whole lot of weeds in my hair.'

He isn't bad at talking to people once he gets down to it. He puts on this very pally expression and they tell him practically anything. Nearly every party there he is with this pally expression listening to some dope and them telling him the secrets of their hearts. I don't think he wants to hear the secrets of their hearts. He's just got this face people tell things to. Honestly they just see his face and make straight for it. Poor old boy I think he gets a bit bored sometimes.

After I'd had this dance, being a deb tailed off really. I went on being one officially till the end of that year. But I didn't feel like one much. I didn't feel like anything much. I just felt like someone who has been a beatnik and a deb, and rather bad at both. I didn't know what to be or anything. I didn't want to go on being a deb because I wasn't much good. And I didn't want to be a secretary. So I just kept going to all these parties to stop thinking about anything at all. Honestly if you don't want to think you just have to keep going to millions of parties and you don't have to. I've never seen anyone thinking at a party. I'd have noticed if I had.

My mother was thinking though. Mostly I think she was thinking what to do with me. After a bit she decided I ought to do this model course. To make me more dignified. And to learn to sit down properly. She's very keen on me sitting down properly and my legs looking tidy and things. I don't think they ever will be actually. I don't think she thought they would either, but I suppose it was worth a try. Also I've got these thick eyebrows. I think they got her down.

The first day I went I had to go and talk to a man. He saw what sort of shape I was, so I suppose he guessed I wasn't going to be a model. He asked me if I was shy. I said, no, I wasn't shy, by my legs were untidy. He said they could probably tidy them up. He said they tidied most people's up after they'd been doing this course for a bit. He said he'd seen much worse than mine. Honestly, he said they were quite mild compared to some he'd seen. I was quite cheered I can tell you. You are cheered, you know. If someone's seen legs worse than yours.

All the other girls doing the course were very thin and tall. I was the only one who wasn't. But they were nice. Thin but jokey. They were all going to be models except me.

The first day we had to walk up and down. It sounds easy as anything. But try walking up and down with fourteen thin girls watching. Normally when you're walking you don't think much about it. It's only when you start walking up and down in front of someone you feel loopy. Like when you start thinking about your ears. Day-to-day you don't think much about your ears except to hear through them or something. But when you actually think about an ear, and its shape and what it looks like and the way it's stuck on your head you feel a bit of a nit about it. It's exactly the same when you start walking up and down in front of someone. You suddenly realize you've got two legs and feet on the end and knee-caps and things. It's a bit much.

Practically the whole of a model course you spend walking up and down. When I did it I tried to make jokes so people wouldn't look at the way I was walking. That's all you can do really, make jokes and hope for the best. If you're my shape and you've got my legs. Actually even the thin girls felt loopy walking up and down. They were very good at laughing at my jokes which was nice because they weren't very good jokes.

They also make you walk up and down in front of a mirror and watch yourself. And look at your shape. When I was looking at my shape in the mirror, the woman said,

'You're pear-shaped.'

So I said, 'I hoped I was hour-glass.'

But she said no, I had to face the facts, I was pear-shaped. I was a bit depressed because I hate pears. Specially their shape. Still, if you are you are. Even if I was an old skeleton I'd still be pear-shaped. I expect if someone digs me up in hundreds of years I shall be known as 'the pear-shaped Kensing-dearthal woman'.

There was one super woman who gave us choreography. You do choreography to break down your inhibitions. She liked me because she said I wasn't inhibited. She said it didn't matter about your shape if you were uninhibited. She said people forgot about your shape. Also most of the pear-shaped women she knew were uninhibited, so perhaps that's the compensation.

We spent quite a bit of time putting on make-up and trying out different shapes for our mouths and eyes. It was rather interesting. A lot of people, when they'd finished, you wouldn't have known they were the same person. And without any make-up on at all you wouldn't have recognized any of them. Apparently that's the whole thing about models. They're not meant to have faces. In fact, if you want to be a model, it's no good having a face. If you've already got a face you can never look different. If you haven't got one then you can paint a new one on every other day if you want to. That's why I'd have been no good even if I wasn't pear-shaped. Because I've got a face. Honestly I've got practically every disadvantage you can have. No really. You name it, I've got it.

After we'd spent two weeks walking up and down and breaking down our inhibitions and putting make-up on we had to bring our clothes to model. All different clothes. Sports clothes, day clothes, evening clothes, everything.

I had a pretty embarrassing time with sports clothes. I brought a pair of trousers and a silk shirt to model. And I'd just started modelling them when the woman stopped me.

'I didn't tell you to bring jodhpurs,' she said.

'They're not jodhpurs, they're trousers,' I said.

'They don't look like trousers,' she said, 'they look like jodhpurs.'

'It's the shape of my legs,' I said, but I was very embarrassed I can tell you.

We had to model with an umbrella as well. I kept on stubbing my toe and putting it in the wrong hand, and the woman got furious. She said I was doing it on purpose. She was always telling me I was doing things on purpose. When I glued up my eyes with eyelash glue, she said I did it on purpose. I didn't want to glue up my old eye, I'm just no good at putting eyelashes on with my right hand. I'm left-handed. They never stopped me being left-handed at school, in case it made me more backward. If you're backward already, changing hands could make you retarded practically your whole life. It could even affect the way your brain worked.

The last day of the course we had to put on a show and be given marks by a panel of people. It was pretty funny all these people trying to put on polite faces at all these really maggie clothes everyone was modelling, and pretending not to notice my being pear-shaped. The choreography woman was one of the panel, and she gave me huge winks to cheer me up.

In the end I got quite good marks, which practically killed me. They said I had a good smile, and being pear-shaped wasn't counted against me. They said I couldn't help it.

So there I was, an uninhibited pear-shaped ex-deb with a good smile. I suppose there's worse things to be.

7

Of course I hadn't stopped thinking about a superman. In spite of being a deb and all that. When I got depressed I used to think about that actor. And once when I was attacked by a sex maniac. It's not much fun being attacked by a sex maniac. I can think of more swoony things. It's not the bit when he leaps on you, or the bit when you try to run and your legs don't move. It's the awful way you get haunted afterwards. You keep on thinking *everyone's* going to leap on you. No really. Once it gets dark every man you see seems about to. When I was running away from that old nut case I kept on thinking about that actor. Mostly because of this innocence he had I suppose. Like you think about something beautiful in the dentist.

When I got really suicidal I used to sit around and think I'd probably never meet anyone like that again. I thought I'd probably end up being a spinster. And everyone saying poor-dear-it's-a-very-sad-story-she-was-disappointed-in-love. You know how they do. Or I thought I'd probably have to be a maiden aunt. Actually I could never decide which was worse, being a maiden aunt or marrying a weed. If you don't find a superman that's about the only choice you've got. Or being an eccentric. I think I'd go in for being an eccentric if I didn't find a superman. I'd wear a straw hat and live in the south of France. Sometimes I think that'd be better than marrying a superman and becoming disillusioned. People's faces go so funny when they're disillusioned. Their eyes go all small and they spend the whole time thinking someone's doing them out of something. And saying I'm-not-such-a-fool-as-I-look-oh-no. And waving their fingers in your face.

Anyway though I didn't have a superman to swoon over I had a good collection of weeds. The one I liked best was this terribly rich one. I hate to think about it now but I really did like him. I mean it's no good pretending I didn't like him because I did. You get all these girls who fall in love with drips, find out they're drips, and then go round swearing they weren't in love with them, they just felt sorry for them. I wasn't in love with this rich weed; he just amused me. I think I liked him best because he was the richest and he had this oil well. And he thought being rich was a joke. It's no good having an oil well if you don't split your sides about it. That's the trouble; most people take them frightfully seriously. They really think it's frightfully serious being rich and having an oil well.

I've forgotten where I met him, this rich weed. Anyhow he used to take me out quite a lot. My grandmother thought he was swoony. Anyone rich is swoony to her. No, I'm not being mean. That's just how she thinks. I mean, she doesn't *only* like rich people, she likes poor people too, but rich people have this particular appeal to her. She liked it when he sent me huge bunches of flowers and presents. She said that was what she understood.

We spent a good deal of the time drinking champagne. I thought you could never get tired of drinking champagne. But you do. Everyone swooned when I drove up with him. They wouldn't have swooned if I'd come by myself. It was the oil well they were swooning about. I know it's corney but I never realized till then that people really minded about money. Not really cared for it. But they really do. It doesn't matter if you're some frightfully rich fiend in human shape; if you give them a big tip they'll smile and practically kiss your feet. I think it's a bit frightening. Because supposing you become a fiend, if you're frightfully rich, no one tells you, and you just go on being a fiend till you die. It makes you think.

Old Cecil – he was called Cecil this rich weed – was on his way to being a fiend when I met him. But I didn't notice it at first. Of course he didn't have a chin or anything. But when you've been a deb you don't expect people to have chins. I mean a chin is a rare luxury. Not something you come across just like that. And the thing is, if you use your imagination, you can pretend they've got chins. And Cecil could be amusing. At the beginning anyway when I hadn't heard any of his jokes. When I was hearing them the second time round it wasn't so easy to imagine he had a chin. That often happens to me actually. I think some-one's really amusing; then when I've been out with them a couple of times I realize they've just got these four or five jokes they tell you, and that's all. Except for these jokes they're hell's boring.

What got me down about Cecil in the end was him telling me about his mistresses and looking flabby. I can't bear chinless people talking about sex. I think all chinless men should be eunuchs. I don't mind if they propose to me, that's quite jokey-jokey, but when they look all flabby and start telling me about their mistresses and talking about sex I want to heave. I couldn't stand it when Cecil went on like that. I used to start talking to the waiters or the people at the next table or something. Once when he just wouldn't stop I sang a hymn.

I think I went on going out with him because I didn't like to disappoint my grandmother. She really enjoyed the oil well and everything so much it was selfish to stop. But it was really tor-ture in the end. He became more and more of a fiend. He didn't care about all the millions of people who were stomping all over England ruining it. And when I burst into tears he said, didn't I want to house the workers? I said, workers nuts, they just care about their old bank balance. And wearing their corney diamond bracelets at lunchtime and stuffing their faces with *pâté*. For heaven's sake you can't eat more than four meals a day.

You can keep your old oil well and yachts and everything. My grandmother thinks I'm mad. No, honestly, M.D. Specially when I stopped going out with old Cecil. She said she couldn't understand it. When I said his chin got me down and he made me feel sick when he talked about sex, she said that sort of atti-tude wouldn't get me anywhere.

I got a temporary job when I left secretarial college. My brother said I needed the experience. The thing was I owed him a whole lot of money. So he was pretty keen on me getting ex-perience. I found this agency and they took me on because they didn't have anyone else. They kept on only giving me half my wages by mistake, but they were quite jokey so I didn't really care. Also they said I was their best girl so I felt rather sorry for them.

They sent me to this place that published hymn-books and encyclopedias. They were good hymn-books actually, and you could buy them on the H.P. I shared a room with a woman called Miss Watts, and a Greek boy. I had my own typewriter and typed things on cards with numbers on them. And Miss Watts used to dictate into this tape-recorder and I typed back from it when she'd finished. I was really meant to be working for this man behind a partition, but whenever he wanted me to do something Miss Watts said I was too busy.

It was a tight fit sharing a desk with Miss Watts. But she was quite interesting. She had a brother who grew vegetables and one grandfather who'd been a Mormon. She wasn't a Mormon, she said she couldn't be doing with all those husbands. Because of only having a one-room flat. The Greek boy and me thought this was terribly funny. He had to add up things in books, and if he wanted a bit more money he just took a frightful long time adding up and got paid pounds and pounds for working over-time. When I left he gave me a pair of pink garters with bows on. Miss Watts was thrilled. She said it was the most romantic thing she'd ever heard. I gave her a box of chocolates and she gave me a handkerchief with a dog on. Only she cried so much I had to lend her the dog back to wipe her eyes.

The reason I left was I was meant to be going to stay with this girl in the south of France. Also I'd paid my rotten old brother back his money. This girl was an International Set type. I don't know why she asked me to stay. I think she liked me because I wasn't. It made a change me not being a princess or anything. She had this terribly good-looking mother she absolutely hated. She said she wouldn't have minded her being a drunk and having lovers if she was nicer. But she didn't even make her laugh.

They had a pink villa and Italian servants like on the movies. And lots of princes and kings staying. That was another thing. This girl's mother was mad on kings. Honestly, you'd only got to say you were a king and she'd swoon. She wasn't too keen on me not being in oil or being a princess, but she put up with it. We spent most of the day on the beach or water skiing, and then in the evenings we went to night clubs after dinner. They were pretty grim. Nearly all the men had bald heads. No honestly.

When you looked round all you saw was bald heads everywhere. Even girls my age were dancing with bald heads. A lot of them were married to them too. Apparently their mothers sold them to the first rich lech that came along. My girl friend, she was terrified she'd get sold too. There was this American who kept on asking her to marry him. He didn't have a bald head but it wouldn't be too long. And her mother was dying for her to marry him. She wasn't in love with anyone else but she didn't want to marry him. I mean I know supermen end up with bald heads but it's pretty stiff starting off with one.

I met an Italian prince while I was there. He was called Carlo. Actually I've never met one that wasn't called Carlo. He wasn't amusing, but he amused me. He was typical old Roman playboy type. The sort the old Borgias chewed up for breakfast. Anyway I used to dash about in his sports car with him, and he took me to the casino and places.

But it was hell if you were on the beach with him because he had these huge biceps. And he did nothing but flex them all the time. He thought everyone on the beach was probably swooning about his old muscles, so he stood about flexing them and then walked up and down frightfully slowly swinging his hips in one of those men's bikinis. I practically died every time he did it. I used to hide behind the lilo and pretend I wasn't with him. But then he'd come and stand in front of me and breathe in and out very slowly. I think he thought I was probably swooning too. If I pretended not to notice him he'd dive into the sea and swim up and down with a snorkel on. He was really embarrassing. Most of the time he was all right though.

One thing about the International Set, they're like beatniks. No one's normal. I suppose being a king and things is a bit of a strain. And Oedipus and all those chaps were pretty royal. I mean it's not often you get peasants being in love with their mothers or obsessed by anything in particular. They swoon over old nymphs flitting about woods and things but it's not often they're incestuous. Anyway I shouldn't think you could go round with the International Set if you were normal. It's no good just being in oil or being a princess; you've got to be perverted or obsessed too. Not only that, you've got to be bored stiff at being perverted or obsessed. It's no good enjoying it. 'Course if you're a princess, in oil, perverted and obsessed, you're in clover. You can't fail. It's not often that happens. Sometimes, but not often.

Another thing you've got to be perverted in the right places, like Montego Bay or Cannes. It's no good doing anything like that in the wrong places. There's practically a special date when it begins. Like grouse shooting or anything else. You know: 11th March, incest begins. Also no one at your school should have been normal. Unless they were all complete queers your small talk will be nil. You can get over that though if your butler's really a woman. It's not as good, mind you, but nearly.

I got on quite well with these kings actually. I think it was such a change me being normal. No really. I think they were fascinated because I was normal. 'Course I didn't stay long enough for them to get bored of me being normal. They probably would have.

When I got home my cousin went off to be a nurse. It was pretty lonely her going off. I missed her a lot. She's good company and everything and we shared a room at school and all that, and once she was a nurse I never saw much of her. She's the sort of person you like to be with. I mean she laughs all the time. I like people who laugh all the time, you get jolly few girls who laugh a lot. They're usually too busy taking their sex appeal seriously. They take their sex appeal so seriously they hardly ever think about how funny everything is. Especially their sex appeal. That's the funniest bit of all.

She used to do this thing, my cousin. Mostly when we were at school. Though once she did it when we were staying in an hotel. She used to make me cover my mouth in lipstick, and she would too. I mean you had to really smear it on. Then we divided up the mirror into two halves and gave it huge kisses, and then we'd see whose mouth was the biggest. She always won. I think that's why she played. And on bath nights at school we dressed up as tarts or Grecian statues. Never anything else because when you've got just sheets you're a bit limited. Unless you're Julius Caesar. And it's not much fun being Julius Caesar. I mean you can't do much when you're Julius Caesar. Except drop dead or write long letters home from Gaul about woad.

We were never jealous of each other because we were so different. It's frightfully boring when you get people being jealous of each other. Particularly if they're jealous of you. I mean *anything* you've got they make you feel guilty about it. For heaven's sake, they make you feel guilty about being alive. I had this girl who was a deb with me like that. If she came to see me, she'd spend the whole time counting my invitations or my dresses or something. I think that's the only reason she came. She never talked to me till she'd finished thumbing through everything. Then if I'd got a single thing she hadn't she'd practically kill me, or look terribly sad. I can't bear that. When people go all droopy and sad. I know it's phoney because as soon as they get what they want you don't get a droop out of them. My mother does that sometimes. She doesn't get furious and shout, which is quite all right. She goes all quiet and sad. Specially when you owe her money.

Anyway after my cousin was a nurse I didn't have anyone to dress up like a tart with. Not that I wanted to particularly. It's just nice to be able to just in case. I suppose I could have had lipstick competitions with someone else, but it's not the same thing really. I don't know why it isn't it just isn't.

It happens all the time really. I mean people going off and doing other things. Or they become completely different. That's worse. I mean it gives you an awful turn. One minute there they are gay and funny and the next time you see them they've become absolute gloom-pots. Except people who become nuns: they always look much happier. That's the sign of someone holy. Not long faces and rosaries. Like the girls at school who spent their whole life in church, and were always the first to live in sin or something corney.

I worked in a pool when I came back from the south of France. It was a pool belonging to a chemical firm. The pool is where they put all these girls to type. You all sit in rows and there's an old woman of about forty who sits and watches you to see you're working. We all had these tape-recorders, so you typed with earphones on. I really enjoyed it. It was like one of those old movies with Cary Grant. And he sees someone fabulous made a mistake you just said, it wasn't you, it was the girl who typing away in the pool and marries her and gets promotion. All the girls were frightfully nice, and lent you things. And if you was away.

They didn't even mind when they found out that my father was a lord. A lot of people mind terribly. They become awfully peculiar with you, or they spend the whole time asking you if he eats or has a bath, or if he's ever been on a train. And when you say yes, he does have a bath, and he spends most of the morning there reading the Flutters, they don't believe you. Or they hate you. No honestly. They hate you before you've even opened your mouth and they hate you doubly more than they hate anyone else. If you're working for them they get much more furious with you than any other person because they think you think you're superior to them. They really think you *think* that. There's nothing you can do about it, because they think it before they even *know* you. And if you do anything like making a joke or looking happy, you're thinking you're better than anyone else. Honestly, you've had it from the start.

But none of the girls in the pool minded. They just went on being exactly the same. Me and the girl who sat next to me called Deborah used to play jet fighters with our earphones. I'd be Jeff Duke and she'd be someone else and we'd make jet noises and do morse code on our typewriters. It wasn't a very intellectual game but it helped to make the time go quicker. And when the supervisor shouted at us we'd pretend not to hear and make extra loud jet noises. I was sad to leave that chemical firm. It's funny the places you feel sad to leave. But I enjoyed those earphones.

After that I went to work in this advertising agency. I was secretary to someone different every week. Everyone in advertising is ex-something. Ex-actors, ex-artists, ex-writers, and quite a few ex-people too. There's two things they all mind about: the Client and Sex. It made me pretty depressed all these people being ex-something. I'd rather someone was a bad writer in one room than thinking up sexy ads for morons. I'm sure his wife wouldn't but I would: 'Course if you tell people that, they think you're boring as hell.

There was one young man I liked in this advertising agency. He was really nice. No, honestly, it wasn't sex, he was just nice and intelligent. We used to have chats about books and things. Everyone thought he was flirting with me or something corney. You can't even say hello when people are sex-conscious and you're in bed. They just don't admit to anything *not* being sex. They don't want anything not to be sex. I mean they practically *die* if everything's not sex. And they practically kill themselves with boredom if you talk about anything else. So if they see you talking to someone they don't want to think you're doing something and not getting a thrill.

I don't think anyone liked me at that advertising agency actually. I can't think of anyone at the moment who did. I don't know. But I think it was basically because I wasn't swoony about sex. It's always going to be a disadvantage. Me not being swoony about sex. Most people are. And they don't like it if you're not. I don't know why. I mean I don't mind them swooning. It's just I can't swoon myself. Except if you're in love. That's different. But most people who swoon about sex aren't in love. And a lot of people who say they're in love are really swooning about sex.

When I'd finished at that advertising place Migo and I went and sailed at this place in Sussex. It was my mother's idea. She's got this great thing that you should always do everything. She never stops thinking up new games she thinks I should play. In case I get asked and can't play them. She has nightmares about me getting asked to play things and not being able to. So now I can do practically everything badly. I can even play Chinese cribbage. No one else can.

Migo and I went sailing with this man with a beard. He was very nice. A lot of men with beards are. My mother doesn't like men with beards. She says she doesn't know what they're hiding and it makes her nervous. Also she says imagination boggles what must get stuck in them. You don't know what you might not find there. Anyway that's what she says. I don't know that I agree with her.

We had long conversations with this man with the beard. About practically everything. It's rather splendid. Sailing along

78

in the sunshine talking about Freud and things. I was no good at sailing. But my mother doesn't mind if I'm not *good* at things. Just so long as I can *do* them. She says people have it over you if you can't do things. She says they sneer at you behind your back. I don't mind if people sneer at me. But she does. My grandmother says that's what happens if you sleep with a man. They've got it over you.

Also just after that one of our castles got emptied. It was sold when I was about nine but most of the stuff got left there. So anyway they sent it over for us to sort it out. It was quite a sight. You try emptying a castle and putting it in a dining-room. It's funny how quickly it goes. I mean one minute there are castles and footmen and coronets and all that, and the next there you are stomping about among lavatory brushes and coroneted napkins, and that's all that's left. It gave me a strange feeling. Because when you see all your castle sitting in your dining-room you jolly well know that everything like that's finished now. And if you don't realize it's all finished now, you've had it. You get weeded out. No honestly you do. I know lots of people and they just can't cope because they don't want to realize it's finished. They won't let themselves realize it.

There were lots of miniatures of ancestors with smug expressions. It made you wonder what it must have been like then. Because they never doubted they were marvellous. And of course owning so much stuff only made them think it all the more. Actually my grandmother's like that. She's absolutely sure she's better than a whole lot of people. Not in a nasty way at all. She's just quite sure about it. No one's like that now. I mean no one's even sure about the whole *world* being better, for heaven's sake. I suppose it's old-fashioned to be sure.

8

I've got a fixation about the Japanese. I've never met anyone
else who has. I don't know where I got it from. I once asked my
father if we have any Japanese blood. He didn't seem to think so.
He said you didn't get much Japanese population in Western
Ireland. He's a bit Buddhist my father. Very philosophical and
all that. Anyway my mother asked this Japanese poet who lived
in Paris to dinner once. Honestly he was swoony. He talked about
being madly Zen, which I knew about. On account of being an
ex-beatnik. And he did all this Japanese painting on silk and
arranging one flower on a bit of bark. Actually most Japanese
arrange things on bark I suppose, but he was the first one I'd
had dinner with. I knew some in Paris but I never had dinner
with them. I think what's fascinating about them is they're
inscrutable, like the Chinese at the Sorbonne. I mean you don't
know what they're thinking about.

After the Japanese had been to dinner he wrote and asked me
to have dinner with him, we went to a Chinese restaurant in the
King's Road. He chose all the food. All really genuine Oriental
stuff; no Americanized dishes. It was very interesting of course,
but I prefer the ordinary old sweet-sour this and that and bean
sprouts. Mind you, my mother says I'm the sort of person who'd
rather eat Ticky Snack pies and tomato ketchup than anything
else. My father's a bit like that. He's always having bread and
dripping when my mother's not looking.

Anyway we had this dinner, and talked some more about
Buddha and cherry blossom. There is quite a lot to say about
Buddha and cherry blossom. He told me about his father who
was a Buddhist scholar and then he asked me to come and listen
to a record in his flat. I said all right because it seemed a bit
rude to say no. Half-way there I did begin to get a bit nervous

though. It was in the taxi really. He didn't look so inscrutable. I mean I think I did know what he was thinking about after all.

He had one of those terribly quiet flats. With lights over the pictures and a deaf housekeeper somewhere. I sat on the sofa and he put on a record and asked me to dance with him. I didn't want to in the least. I like dancing, but not just by myself in someone's flat. Well, not with a friend of my mother's anyway. Besides he was quite old. I suppose for one glorious evening he'd *forgotten* he was.

I didn't want to hurt his feelings. I mean I thought perhaps it was an old Japanese custom to dance after dinner. But I said I thought I'd like to listen to his record for a bit first. And then maybe dance later. So we sat and listened to this record. Him at one end of the sofa and me at the other. Then he said, could he recite me one of his poems? So he did, and while he was reciting it kept on moving closer and closer till I was practically flattened against the side of the sofa. Then he said I was like a cherry blossom blowing in a spring breeze. I said, what gave him *that* idea, and he said he'd thought it ever since he'd first seen me. He said he supposed he couldn't ever hope that the cherry blossom could be his, could he? I thought not. I really did. To tell you the truth I was nervous, not to say worried. It can be a bit worrying with only a deaf housekeeper about. I mean you can't help thinking, supposing he tries to pick the blossom for himself?

We had a bit of an argument about me being cherry blossom. I said I thought the cherry blossom's mother might be anxious about her. He calmed down a bit then. My mother's no laughing matter sometimes, so it helps every now and then to mutter about her if you're a bit in dickie's meadow. He looked very sad when I pretended to worry about my mother. He said it would always be the tragedy of his life that I was forbidden fruit. It seemed to have come on autumn suddenly. I said, yes, it was pretty tragic. So any way little forbidden old me got in a taxi and went home. My mother screamed with laughter when I told her. She'd warned me about Japanese etchings; how was I to know they would turn into just the old jazz – with Brubeck? Still, it's all good experience.

About this time they all got into a bit of a thing about what sort of a job I should do. They said I had to settle down and do a proper job. Only no one could think of what I could do. Mostly because of me not being very bright. There aren't many jobs about for girls who aren't bright, and no good at shorthand. I mean I can do it. But I'm no *good* at it. The thing is most girls are either bright and don't do shorthand or dumb and marvellous-at-shorthand. It's not often you get girls who can't do anything, like me. And when you do, jobs for them are a bit limited, I can tell you.

What I did was to go to all these agencies and they gave me jobs to go and see. But, you see, it was the same thing everywhere. They wanted you to be either clever or good at shorthand. It was a bit depressing. I mean you feel a bit of a failure when no one wants you. Not that you blame them not wanting you. I mean, if I interviewed me, I don't think I'd want me either. In fact I'm sure I wouldn't. Most of all what's wrong with me is I talk and make jokes. I can't help it. It's a nervous habit with me. Every time someone asks me what I like doing or what I can do, I start making jokes. Psychologically I suppose it's because I'm trying to cover up that I can never think of *anything* I like doing, let alone anything I actually *can* do. I can only think of things I'd like to do if I was someone else. Not many people want to know about that. Not when they're looking for a secretary or something anyway.

It makes you pretty depressed really. Feeling a failure. You just go on and on seeing all these people. You can feel they don't like the look of you and they say polite things about getting in touch with you later. And however you dress you're wrong. If you wear a camel-haired coat, they think they don't want a dreary bag like you in their office, and, if you look smart and with it, they think it might be dangerous to have a tarty piece among the files. You can't help wondering what it must be like if you had a sick mother and really needed the job. Not being clever or good at shorthand you'd be worried I can tell you. I was only worried because my father was getting a bit bored of paying my bills and me being a failure. I didn't have a sick mother or anything.

It would have been all right if there had been another failure in the family. You could just say you took after them, but all my family aren't failures. I was the only one. That's the worst thing about being a failure, being alone. My father says it's the same thing when you're a martyr. You're alone. You feel such a ninny being tortured all by yourself. It's not so bad if you're singing and holding palms with lots of other martyrs. Being by yourself is the worst thing.

I've forgotten how many jobs I went for. Millions and millions anyway. Then I went to this one which was a woman who wanted a secretary. She was a pretty funny-looking, very tall woman, quite jokey but with these very glittery eyes. Anyway, she hadn't talked to me for five minutes when she said she'd have me. I was pretty flattered I can tell you. When you've been practically everywhere hoping people will like you, you're pretty flattered when someone likes you after only five minutes. I thought she was probably terribly acute. My mother couldn't believe it. She was really thrilled. She thought at last I was going to stop being a failure.

The job was helping this woman run a shop in Hampstead for these different kinds of writing paper. She was in charge of the shop, and also there was one other man. I had an office and my own typewriter and telephone. Pretty important. And the woman was terribly nice. She was always coming in and having little chats with me, and I arranged the shop in a different way and she said it was the best it had ever been done and I must have an artistic nature. I'm a sucker for people telling me I'm artistic. Honestly, you've only got to tell me I'm artistic and I swoon. I never believe anything else people say to me, only when they say I'm artistic. I suppose it's because I'm not and I'd like to be. Rather sad.

I had to take a bit of dictation from this man as well. He was pretty ghastly. I mean you felt sorry for him, but he was still ghastly. You know what he looked like. He looked like a monkey with one of those hangy upper lips. And he used to suck it after every comma. His lip I mean. Honestly, all the time, comma, suck, comma, suck. It got you down it really did. He was terrified of this other woman. I couldn't understand it. Every time she went into his office he'd start scratching and shaking all over the place even when she rang him up he'd start shaking. I thought he was nuts. I mean, this woman, there was something funny about her, but she was quite jokey most of the time.

They had salesmen selling suitcasefuls of samples of this writing paper all round the country, and at the beginning of every month they'd stomp in and go over all their stuff with the man and this woman. They waited in my office till she called them in. You know what. They went on just like that nitty man, shaking up and down and chain-smoking. It really got me down seeing these men twitching all over the place. And all they'd got to do was have a little chat and go over their stuff with her. After a bit I asked one of them why he was in such a state, and he said it was because this woman hated men.

I didn't think much about this woman hating men. I just thought I was lucky being a girl, because I didn't have to twitch every time she spoke to me. In fact she became nicer and nicer to me. Really swoony. I'd never worked for a woman before who was so nice to me. She took me shopping with her and had coffee with me and everything. I couldn't get over it. I thought at last I'd found my vocation in life.

It was swoons all round till one afternoon when I was helping her count up all this writing paper and check it off on a list. I couldn't understand why she kept on bumping into me. And then laughing. I mean, there I was humming away counting up all this stuff, and the next minute she'd bump into me from behind and give this funny laugh. Then we were in this large cupboard under the stairs counting up more of this stuff and she started pushing me into these piles of writing paper, and her eyes looked all starey.

Do you know it never clicked till then. I told you I was dumb. I mean she'd got these funny eyes, but nothing else. Lesbians aren't my swooniest subject. I suppose it was rather funny actually. Her chasing me round this cupboard and all these stacks of writing paper. I found it a bit difficult to laugh though. What I did do was, I dashed out of that cupboard and was sick in the loo.

Of course after that she was absolutely foul. I suppose lesbians are the same as men. I mean if you refuse to sleep with a man he's always terribly rude to you. And I realized why all those men twitched all the time. I asked one of them why he didn't leave. But he said he couldn't, he didn't think he'd find another job. He was dumb like me, and also he was fifty and had three children. He said she knew that. That's why she could be as foul as she liked. I hope she burns in hell. Honestly, I really do. If you'd seen those poor dumb salesmen twitching you would too.

What happened in the end was that she sacked me the same time as I gave in my notice. My mother was furious. The thing was, I was back where I started. Being a failure again. And it can be pretty nerve-racking having a failure stomping round the house. I couldn't tell her about this old girl being a lesbian, because I didn't want to talk about it. When something like that happens I can't talk about it for ages afterwards. I don't know why I can't, it's pretty po-faced of me. But I just can't. I was the same when that sex maniac leapt on me.

Actually I should have been warned by those glittery eyes. My mother says they all have them. Terribly hard glittery eyes. I know one when I see one now. But I didn't then. If I did I wouldn't have taken that job.

I didn't start looking for another job. We were all too bored about me being a failure to be able to think about it for a bit. I started writing this really corney novel. I used to wear this red flannel nightdress to write in. I couldn't write a word unless I had this nightdress on. That's what I did practically all the time. Write this corney novel or spend hours looking at myself in the mirror. No honestly. I spent hours and hours looking at myself and having long conversations with myself. Well, it wasn't always just with myself; sometimes I'd pretend I was talking to someone else. Most of the time I just talked to myself though. You probably think I'm nuts. But I know millions of people who spend a lot of time talking to themselves in mirrors. It's not only me that does it. Actually I still have conversations with myself walking along the street. It can be pretty lonely walking along the street and you don't notice it so much if you have a conversation with yourself. The time goes much quicker.

I was in the middle of writing this novel when I met a swoony man at a party. It was one of those literary parties where everyone spends the whole time asking you if you can write. And you spend the whole time telling them the plot of some corney novel you're writing, and then they tell you the plot of the corney novel they're writing. That's all that happens. It's just everyone going round telling each other corney plots. I was in the middle of listening to someone's plot when I noticed this neck. I think you can tell what a man's like just by looking at his neck. This neck was pretty swoony. And so was the man actually. He had a Grecian nose and very brilliant eyes. I suppose those sort of eyes are old hat. But you know the kind that look at you. I mean you really know they're looking at you and no one else. Most people's eyes could be looking at anyone. It's unusual when people look just at you.

He wrote scripts for movies, this man. He didn't tell me about them, but I think they were good scripts. We went out to dinner after this literary party. Honestly he was fascinating. I mean once he started looking at you you'd be all mesmerized. Say you were taking a mouthful of soup, if he started looking at you. Your spoon would get stuck. Absolutely frozen in your mouth. You didn't want to be mesmerized but you just were.

Once he took me to a concert at the Festival Hall, and I felt extraordinary sitting next to him. He kept his eyes on the orchestra and you really thought he was going to turn them to stone. I used to wonder if he had an aunt who was a witch. It wouldn't have surprised me a bit if he'd been a black magic dabbler. It really wouldn't. He was very imaginative of course. I mean he could talk away and interest you and he had a chin. It's marvellous going out with a chin when you hardly ever do. Also when you were with him everything was very exciting. Even walking along a road. When you walked along a road with him it was really exciting. Not corney exciting but sort of vital.

You couldn't fall in love with him though. He was fascinating, but you couldn't love him. You were mesmerized but not swooning. It was a good thing actually, because he was married.

I didn't know he was married. He didn't tell me for ages. It didn't shock me. Him being married. I think he wanted it to. I don't know why. It was the way he told me somehow.

Actually I was steaming up his car window and drawing faces on it when he told me. So I went on steaming it up and drawing faces. Then I just said I didn't think I could go on going out with him. He said, 'Why?' So I said it was against my principles. I've never found out what principles are exactly, but, if I've got any, not going out with married men is one of them. I've got one girl friend I don't think has ever been out with someone single. She says married men are more mature. They understand her better. Also they're more experienced. Anyway old married boots was a rotter. Not fundamentally decent. It was a good thing I wasn't in love with him. I might have been mad about him. I mean it wasn't his fault I wasn't.

I was a bit preoccupied with weeds actually. I suppose it was because I wasn't working or anything. You get a bit one-track-minded. Everyone's got to be mad on you or you nearly die. The thing is you keep hoping that one of these weeds will turn out to be a superman. There was one man, I thought he was a superman for three days. Honestly I was swooning about him for three days. He rang me up all day long and we used to talk for hours and hours. It really got my father down. I don't know what he'd have done if I'd been mad on him for more than three days. It was pretty embarrassing when I wasn't mad on him the fourth day actually. I don't know why but suddenly I just wasn't. He asked me if I loved him in a coffee bar, and I said yes, with my fingers crossed under the table. I don't think it's a lie if you have your fingers crossed. And I couldn't say I wasn't. I really couldn't. Not when I'd been swooning just the day before. You feel such a nit.

It was a shame I wasn't in love with him longer, because he was nice. He was very d. indeed and not a bit a rotter. I didn't actually tell him I wasn't in love with him; he just sort of gathered. I think really what it was, it was his trousers. I didn't look at his legs the first three days. He was quite amusing so there wasn't any need to. I mean if someone's talking away to you you don't usually look at their legs. Then when I saw him the fourth day I suddenly noticed. His legs I mean. Well, not his actual legs, but his trousers. They were huge square things. Enormous square baggy billowy things. I couldn't swoon any more after that. I wanted to but I just couldn't. For heavens sake, they were like the things my father wears. My father's all right, but not even his best friend could say he had swoony legs.

What that man did do, though. He cured me of having a complex about my hips. I've got these huge hips. No really. Enormous. And he liked them. I mean, he said they weren't ugly a bit, and suddenly I didn't mind about them any more. I did before. I used to keep my coat on for hours and hours because I thought everyone would die if they saw them. At parties I'd keep it on the whole evening in case no one would talk to me if they saw them. And I did anything to make people walk out of restaurants in front of me. No really. I'd say anything rather than have them walk behind me, and if they did I could feel their eyes boring into my back. And I thought they probably felt terribly sorry for me, and went on seeing me from pity. But that man he even went on liking them after he'd seen me in a swim-suit. 'Course he might have been blind with love, but I was too thrilled to think of that. It's marvellous when you stop minding about things. Specially about your hips. Anyway they're such big things to mind about. Honestly, you should see them.

9

I think me being hours on the telephone to that man really got my father down. Anyway he decided that finally he had to get me off his mind. And earning money. So he wrote to this office he knows very well and said, did they want any more secretaries? And they said yes. So I filled in all those forms they make you fill in. You know. What sex? What sex your parents? Are they sure? Are you a vampire? All that. Then this woman wrote and asked me to come for an interview. Only because she knew my father I think. Anyway I went.

Interviews are just as bad as you think they're going to be. First of all you don't know what to wear, then when you get there you can't remember whether you ate onions for lunch, so you spend the whole time mumbling sideways in case you did. Then you know you're going to hiccup so you have to cover it up with a coughing fit, and they ask you if you've had a medical, and, if you haven't, look doubtful about whether you're T.B. And, when they tell you about what sort of job it is, you know you're going to hate every minute of it. And they usually say they only take on nice girls. So you try and look madly nice, and know you're going to loathe all the other nice girls. Sometimes I think I'd rather be a tart than go to another interview. Still I suppose even if you're a tart you have to be interviewed by a pimp. So you're back where you started.

By the time they said yes they would have me, it was the last thing I wanted to do, be a secretary in that old office. I nearly died when they said they'd have me. Still, my father was pushing really hard, so I'd had it. Anyway there's always the chance you might get run over on your way there. Or have a heart attack on the bus.

The first morning I went there that's what I did. I sat on the bus praying I'd have a heart attack. I didn't have one though, I spent most of the morning filling in more forms, then they sent me off to have lunch with this girl. I didn't know what to say to her. We had this ham salad so I talked about ham for quite a lot of the time. I could see she wasn't interested in ham, but I couldn't think of anything else.

Then we stomped along to this room where all these secretaries worked. And she introduced me to them all, one by one. They all tried to look as if they weren't very interested, but I knew they were. Not nice interested either. I knew they were all hating me before I even said hello, because they knew who my corney old father was. Honestly you die inside when you know people are hating you, because nothing you say seems to sound all right. So you end up not saying anything. Just smiling vacantly at your typewriter.

This girl who was in charge started telling me very quietly in a corner what the work was about, and what I had to do and everything. But I couldn't hear a word she was saying. The thing was she was saying all these things very quietly into my deaf ear. I've got this deaf ear, and when people say things very quietly into it I can't hear a thing. I didn't dare say I couldn't hear a thing she was saying. I thought she'd probably think I was being too grand to listen. So I sat the whole afternoon nodding and agreeing and not hearing a word. Honestly it was really embarrassing. Specially the next morning when I couldn't understand a word of what I was doing.

The first week they didn't put me to work for anyone. They just gave me things to type and letters to copy. That was embarrassing too, because I could only type terribly slowly because I hadn't done a job for such ages. And I knew they were all watching to see how fast I was going. So after every two lines I'd look round and give this shaky laugh. You try it, honestly it's no joke. Typing and giving shaky laughs all day long. You just think you'll never be able to stop. You think you're going to be there sweating and typing for the rest of your life. No really. Your whole life.

One thing about this office. They had terribly long coffee and tea breaks. Not just a cup at your desk, you went to this room and sat at tables and everything. 'Course the first week I was there no one much spoke to me, so I went to coffee and tea every day with these same two girls. It was much worse than typing. Honestly I used to sit there longing to be back sweating at my typewriter. The thing was I knew they were just dying to get me out of the way and say a few splendidly catty things about me and my typing. Only they couldn't because I was there and they were meant to be seeing I had someone to have coffee with.

You should have heard what they did talk about, these two girls. It was fantastic – day after day. They talked about how they washed their cardigans. And once they'd washed them they asked each other if they'd shrunk, and whether they should iron them. It wasn't that they couldn't talk about anything else, they just didn't want to. If I sort of murmured about something else they carried on talking about these old cardigans as if I wasn't there. Once I asked one of them if she had a boy friend, and she looked so offended you'd think I'd asked her if she was still a virgin. It would have killed me if she hadn't been. Though actually it's often the po-type girl that's swooniest about sex. They sit about looking very respectable and the next minute they're buying a smock.

'Course it's the old, old story when you get bags of women all working on top of each other. They just sit about knitting and talking about each other. If they haven't much imagination that's all they can think of doing. And once they've been doing it for a long time they couldn't stop if they wanted. Also they get this thing, like people in prison. They mind passionately about the tiniest things. Even things like whose turn to shut the window. And quarrel like anything for hours before they decide. It really matters to them whose turn it is. I don't think it does in the beginning, but I suppose after a bit they just get like everyone else. And they are in a prison. Only not the kind you can get out of.

None of those women liked me. I didn't really blame them. I don't think I'd have liked me if I'd been them either. It was awful at first because it was so lonely. When you've been a failure you mind about people not liking you. It really worries you. Because you're just a different kind of failure. But still a failure. Do you know I used to sit having coffee with those women, and sometimes I really wondered if we were all speaking English. No really. I could have been speaking Eskimo for all they knew or cared. And the awful thing was there was so many of them, and only one of me. You can scream with laughter if you've got someone else, but it's practically impossible to laugh by yourself. Every now and then I did though. Very privately behind my typewriter. But it was hardly living it up. I mean I can think of things I've done that were gayer.

Still, you can only mind about things up to a point. Once you've really done your nut about them, they cease to matter any more. Even being lonely you get like that. You mind like anything, then suddenly it just seems splendidly funny and you'd rather die than not be alone among a lot of tiny-minded women. I got more and more eccentric when I was in that office. I had to prove the whole day long that I wasn't like them. Honestly I'd have gone about naked to prove to myself I wasn't. Because every now and then I used to have awful nightmares that I was like them. Or I was becoming like them. Or I would become like them any minute. I'd wake up and find myself knitting and talking about Miss Smith's green hair. Gradually it would creep up on me. I wouldn't know it was happening but one day I'd wake up and I'd be a pretty old thing sniping away making some poor little spotty secretary's life a misery. That's a feminine art that some women have to perfection. It's funny, it's nothing you can put your hand on. They don't swear and scream at you, but very quietly they make you suicidal. And yet you couldn't say what it was. You really couldn't. It's like that tap-dripping torture. I mean, what's an old tap dripping away?

Though it was all right for me. I had a cushy time of it compared to some people. I had weeds and parties and jokey parents and no spots. But imagine what it's like if you're weedless and parentless and you go home to your bed-sitter in the evening, only to eat, sleep and then take the tube again to face tiny minds for another eight hours. And on top of that you've got some old bitch sniping away at you. And you can't get another job, because you're afraid. I could have left any day, I only didn't because I wanted to prove I could stay in a job. I mean you feel sorry for those bitches till you see them torturing little asthmatic secretaries with runny noses. Hell, I was fair game.

I nearly went to live with an awful smooth man from working in that office. Honestly I was mad. I mean if you've got to live with someone it really shouldn't be some awful smooth slug. It was all part of proving madly that I wasn't becoming a net-curtain semi-detached typist. I wanted to be a bosomy sex symbol. One of those women from movie posters: 'Men loved and hated her. She was fire to the blood. No man had been known to forget her.'

I don't know why I even felt tempted to live with this slug. Except he wanted me to. But mostly when people ask me I scream with laughter. I didn't with him. He was the first weed who even tempted me. And yet I didn't love him in the least. I suppose I was flattered at being fire to someone's blood. Even a smooth slug. And he couldn't have been smoother. Honestly everything about him. He was good-looking, but in a very smooth way. He was smoothly intelligent, smoothly amusing, smoothly attentive. He had a smooth car and a smooth flat and he smoked smooth cigarettes.

Also he was smoothly seductive. He made you feel very silly because you wouldn't sleep with him. Not furious or anything. Just very silly. Actually it's funny about when men are trying to seduce you. You think up every reason. Like you're religious, your mother wouldn't like it, you respect them too much, all the corniest things. And the one thing you never think of is, you'd rather die than sleep with them and they make you feel quite sick anyway.

But this smooth man didn't make me feel sick. That was the trouble. It would have been easy if he'd made me feel sick. Not only didn't he make me feel sick, he made me laugh. When people make you feel a little foolish and make you laugh too it seems stupid. Particularly sometimes when you feel sad about not finding another superman. It was Migo who stopped me turning into a smooth mistress of a smooth slug. She said imagine if I got smoothly pregnant and had to get smoothly married and live smoothly ever after in that smooth flat. I couldn't take that. I really couldn't. Imagine having a smooth breakfast every morning. And watching him eat smooth boiled eggs. It would kill me.

Then Chloë came to work in this office. She was at school with Migo and me. She was going to be an actress, but she couldn't stand everyone stabbing everyone in the back. Anyway that's what she said. So she got down to being an old secretary like me. It made it much better Chloë being there actually, because she was pretty jokey. She couldn't do shorthand to save her life, and I don't think she knew how to wash a cardigan either. We both worked for two people in the same room, and we'd have secret signs to each other when we were taking dictation. Endless sunny afternoons we'd sit pretending we were in bikinis gambolling on beaches with bronzed men. That's one thing; if you've got imagination, they can never really stop you dreaming. It takes a bit of imagination to pretend you're on a beach when you're doing shorthand.

It really wasn't bad being in that office with Chloë. Once you've got one other person to laugh with you're all right. That's the worst thing whatever you're doing not having someone to laugh with. I should think hell would be all right if you had some other sinner to joke with. You could spend the whole time screaming with laughter at the devil. I bet he's an awful ham anyway.

Chloë went on being very jokey till she fell in love. She fell in love with this frightfully rich man. I felt sorry for her, because it's practically impossible to be jokey when you're in love. Admittedly she wanted to be in love. Most girls do. They don't feel all right unless they're in love or having a broken heart. Chloë never really wasn't in love or broken-hearted when I knew her. When she first started working in that office with me she was broken-hearted. She was being gay and jokey to cover up that her life was ruined. Then once she'd fallen in love again she was happy. She'd got something to suffer about. She used to stay at the office being over-worked when he wasn't taking her out. She sat looking noble and carrying bravely on with shorthand in spite of everything, ages after we'd all stomped home. And she used to lean against the filing-cupboards and sigh. She always looked as if she had drapey things on. She didn't actually. Only scarves and things tied round her which she spent the whole time looping about. Specially on her extra droopy days.

She lived in this flat in Fulham with three other girls. I went and had supper with them once or twice. They were a pretty funny lot. In fact the whole place was pretty funny. It had a funny atmosphere. It hit you when you walked in the door. Not only me. It hit Migo too. She noticed it as well as me. It wasn't Chloë really, it was these other three girls. They prowled about all looking the same. They had this funny look in their eyes. Very nervous and as if they were waiting all the time for something. No really they did.

Migo and I called them the waiting women. 'Course basically they were all just looking around for supermen, I suppose. Only more than most girls. They just didn't think about anything else. Not one other thing. They were just waiting round for the telephone to ring, or the door, or the post. They never actually did anything except wait around. I suppose that's why they had this funny look in their eyes. Chloë was the only one that did anything like a job. I think it made her a bit po being among all those waiting women. She wasn't po naturally. Stagey but not po.

Two of those waiting women were frightfully morbid and nervy. The post was always not going to come, the telephone was never going to ring. It really got me down all the bells that weren't going to ring. And the other one was frightfully smarty-smarty. One has one's hair done at the Queen's hairdresser, one's writing paper from the Queen's stationer, one's weekends in Berks, Bucks or Wilts, and one's weeny runabout to Harrods to meet one's girl friends for lunch. And one swoons over teeny-minded weeds in Knightsbridge flats.

One of those morbid girls told me about this man she was in love with. She was in love with him, for heaven's sake. She actually told me she loved him, and then she said the most disgusting thing I've ever heard about him. Honestly I felt sorry for the man having her in love with him, even if it was true. When I told Chloë she just laughed and said if I knew the man I'd say the same thing. She couldn't understand that it's pretty warped to say things like that about someone you're meant to be in love with. She was funny like that, Chloë. She really was.

She used to tell me about this frightfully rich man. She said being in love with him was like diving into a deep pool. That's what she said. I couldn't understand. I said I thought I'd been in love but I didn't think it was like diving into a deep pool. She said I wasn't mature. She said if I was mature I'd understand. Only mature people understood. She could be pretty boring like that. She used to get frightfully cross with Migo and I when we made jokes. Specially jokes about love. She said making jokes about love was immature.

I went out to lunch with these girls and Chloë every now and then. They all sat in this coffee bar and talked about clothes and hair. That was all right. Then they'd start talking about other girls' clothes and hair. That was really boring. You should have heard them. No one was all right. They always spoiled themselves. Honestly I never heard them talk about someone who was all right all over. They always spoilt themselves with too much make-up or too short skirts, or they were too tarty or too dull. And if they were fat they should go on a diet, and if they were thin then of course men hated girls who were thin like that. And you wouldn't know the poor wretch was a girl at all, if you saw her from behind, you'd think she was a boy. She was just a clothes-peg. And they'd all rather die than be like that. Men liked women to be women.

There was one other thing they talked about. That was who was engaged or married or pregnant. That was pretty funny too. If the man wasn't a drip, then she was getting married because she had to, and everyone knew why she had an Empire-line wedding dress. They'd sit for hours counting up how many months between when she got married and had the baby. And of course it could have been a seven months' baby. But it was pretty funny because they were usually small and someone had seen it and it was huge. That kind of conversation makes me want to be a tart.

Anyhow they decided to share a party with Migo and I and hold it in their flat. We sent millions of invitations to weeds and drips all over London. And they all came. The waiting women were thrilled. It was the only thing they lived for just to have millions of weeds to swoon over. It was going to be a weed feast.

It was the usual sort of bodies-everywhere party that people give in Fulham. Bodies among coats, furniture, glasses, behind the dustbin, in the bath – everywhere. Phoney old eroticism. Routine type. I fell asleep in a cupboard half-way through because someone put something in my drink. I didn't really care because it saved me the boredom of introducing more weeds to more drippy girls. Some girls are so drippy at parties you could die. They either make straight for the food and stand stuffing their faces or sit about telling other girls how awful they think all the weeds are. Or they come looking beautiful and expect everyone to swoon up and talk to them because they're beautiful. By the end you could kill them. I don't know why they come sometimes. Honestly I don't.

When I crawled out of that cupboard the party was practically over. It was pretty funny actually. I mean it's not every day you wake up and find yourself surrounded by dresses and hangers. Then I couldn't get the door open because some couple were having a passionate scene against it. They looked a bit surprised to see me crawl out. Then they just went on having their passionate scene. They weren't the only ones. All over the floor these couples were having great scenes, and in the middle of them sitting up in bed with a nightie on was old Chloë. She had face-cream on and she was putting curlers in her hair. It didn't worry her all these scenes going on. She's good like that. She was going to bed, and that was it. She's very particular about her sleep actually. It really worries her if she doesn't get her right amount. It makes her skin sag. Anyway that's what she says.

I went into the kitchen and found a little spotty man trying to light the oven. Well, turn the gas on anyway. I said, why did he want to turn the oven on? And he said he wanted to put his head in it. I said couldn't he find something else to do, putting your head in the oven isn't a swoony way to spend a party. Even a bad party. He said, no, he had to put his head in the oven, he'd promised someone faithfully that he would. He'd given his word he would. He never went back on his word. Never. I said I hated to make him break his word, but the oven didn't work. So he burst into tears all over the kitchen table, and I gave him a dish-cloth to wipe his tears. Poor little spotty man. I forgot to ask him why he had to put his head in the oven.

Chloë never saw her rich man after that party. So she went back to being bravely happy again. I preferred her being bravely happy to being in love. And the waiting women went back to waiting, and listening for their bells. Nut-case lot. And the awful thing is they'll be worse when they're married. Because when you wait around for something and never think about anything else you're always disappointed. And disappointed married women are hell. They spend the whole time being just thirty, and having shoulder-length hair and reading historical novels. No, it's true. Really. I know lots of women like that. They're the end, they really are.

10

I've always been mad on the theatre. I suppose it's pretty corney. My mother writes plays so it's not surprising really. She's been writing plays ever since I can remember. I used to go and eat kippers with my grandmother because she had to go to rehearsals. When I fell in love with that actor she used to blame herself for it. She said I wouldn't have fallen in love with him if she hadn't written plays.

I don't know a lot of actors. A few but not a lot. Mostly I think they're more amusing than ordinary people. A lot of people still talk about them as if they weren't being buried in holy ground for heaven's sake. Especially my grandmother. She calls them 'theatricals'. Anything she says about them she always says at the end, 'What can you expect of theatricals?' When I used to eat kippers with her she always said, 'I hope your mother doesn't bring any of those theatricals back with her.' And when I said, 'Why?' she said they had filthy habits.

My mother had a play on when I was at school. It was pretty exciting for me. And for the nuns too. They spent the whole time praying it would be a success, but it wasn't. It was very disappointing after all those prayers. What I said to one nun was, perhaps God didn't like the play. You don't know, do you? It just might not have been the kind of thing that made Him laugh. Not His sort of play.

During my holidays my mother often used to take me to see actors and people to try and get them interested in her plays. Mostly they weren't very swoony about them. One or two of them were, but not many. My mother said you couldn't blame them. She said they only really had time to be interested in who was going to put them into plays. She said being an actor wasn't funny. It was sad, really. Because of being out of work, and staying at home waiting for an agent to ring. Also hoping you could pay the phone bill.

My father doesn't swoon about actors. That one I was in love with was the only one he really liked. He looks a bit strange when they call him darling. And he tries to swoon when they tell him about when Bobby lost his wig and Geoffrey had to walk on with the book under the bedpan. But he can't. It's not really *him*. I don't think he'd go to the theatre much if it wasn't for my mother. Anyway he says he hates the intervals. That's why he likes the movies better because there aren't any intervals. He says it's like someone telling you a story and then going off to the loo in the middle.

He has one thing just like me, my father. If he goes to a movie he always comes out *being* whoever he's seen. My mother doesn't. She doesn't understand a bit, she's just going on being herself when she comes out. But my father, if he's seen Hannibal, he's being Hannibal for at least two hours afterwards. Or if he's seen a war movie he's being frightfully stiff upper lip, and I'm the same. If I see some huge sex symbol I'm a huge sex symbol, and if I see some playful sprite then I'm being a playful sprite. It's pretty annoying when my mother goes on being herself though. I mean, if you're being Hannibal, you don't want to be asked to go and get someone's slippers.

Then someone bought another of my mother's plays. And I used to stomp off to rehearsals with her. Watching rehearsals I decided I didn't think I'd like to be an actress after all. I used to think it would be marvellous. I still think it's all right but not marvellous. Everyone's so nervy, and smoky, at rehearsals. I don't think I'd have the guts to act away with everyone being nervy and smoky round me. For heaven's sake, I can't even type with people being nervy and smoky. No honestly I can't. My fingers go all stiff.

Also people seem rather shouty at rehearsals. They don't just say rude words to each other; they shout them. I can't bear people shouting at me. I don't mind if they talk in a loud voice. But, if they shout right at me, my eyes go all watery and I can't do anything. I get like that even when I'm on a horse. No, it's true. If someone shouts at me when I'm on a horse my eyes go all watery and I nearly fall off.

One of the actresses in my mother's play had a daughter about my age. We often got left together, and we used to have little chats. Mostly about the theatre. She was very pretty. More than pretty actually, and more than beautiful. And very nice. Nervous but very nice. She was the only person who was sympathetic when the play was a flop. Not just because her mother was in it either. It's always pretty corney when a play is a flop. Everyone blames everyone else. But she was sympathetic without being corney. Lots of people when they're being sympathetic just make you want to cut your throat.

I didn't see her again for ages and ages, then she suddenly rang me up and came to see me. She was madly in love with a fascinating man, and she chatted away about it. Then she said she was pregnant. Just like that. For heaven's sake, like you'd say, 'Have an olive.' I said, how did she know for sure, and she said she'd been to a doctor. She was going to a psychiatrist and he'd prove her unfit to have a baby, then she'd have an abortion. She'd had a girl friend the same thing happened to. It was dead simple.

I said, please, couldn't she have the baby? Did she *have* to get rid of it? She said, yes, she had to get rid of it, she was too frightened to have it. I couldn't do anything to make her not frightened. I just didn't want her to kill it. I couldn't stop thinking she was getting rid of a her for a me. Because you are. No one seems to think of that. They just think, let's get rid of this annoying thing, and then whoop it up and forget it ever happened. It gets me down, it really does.

And they say all those corney things like, it would only grow up to be miserable. How do they know it would be miserable? It might grow up to be ecstatically happy. Anyway, whatever they say, they're stopping it knowing what it's like to live. Living can be hell but imagine never having lived. Never known a sunny day or laughed or loved anyone. Just been an unwanted thing. Go on, you have a go at being an unwanted thing.

She married the fascinating man about six months after she'd had the abortion. And she had another baby. I saw it the other day and it's very beautiful. It would give me nightmares if it was mine. Honestly it would. I'd keep wondering if the other one was as beautiful. Pretty corney I suppose. Still it depends how you think really. I mean if you don't think like that it doesn't worry you.

It wasn't her fault so much as her mother's. She souped up her having an affair with the fascinating man. She made it seem all right. Glamorous and super. She ought to have been shot.

That girl and her abortion was the first time I realized that you don't live happily ever after. 'Course I knew that some people didn't. But they weren't really people I knew very well. I just always took it for granted that you live happily ever after. My parents have lived happily ever after by and large. They really have. I think my father gets a bit browned off with getting hot-water-bottles for migraines sometimes, and my mother wouldn't mind him being a bit richer, but on the whole they've lived happily ever after.

Not many girls' parents live happily ever after. I only know about two girls' parents who have. Even if they're not divorced or something, they've usually got corney old lovers. Because lovers are corney. They're so corney you could die. Divorce is corney, queers and incest are corney. Someone's going to have to invent something else.

That's the trouble now really. You just can't find anything to do that's going to shock anyone. Honestly, it's pretty miserable not being able to shock anyone. There's nothing you can do that people won't yawn if you tell them about it. You can't even surprise them by being naked. A friend of mine went to a party naked. Nothing on at all. She had her coat on to arrive in but nothing underneath. You'd think people would be a bit surprised but they weren't at all. She said they hardly noticed at all. Mind you, it was quite dark. Even so you'd think they'd be a bit taken aback. She said one person said what a nice pink dress she had on but that's all.

One thing though. I wish fat women were admired now. I do honestly. I wish huge great fleshy women were what men swooned over. I'm not exactly a huge fat woman on the beach. But jolly near. Mostly it's my hips actually. I've got one friend, it's her back. She's thin all over except for this back. I don't think fleshy women will come back. They're just not practical I suppose. What with buses and things. You couldn't get them all on.

Slimming's one of my hobbies really. Migo and I. I should think we've done every diet you can do. Migo's as thin as anything. She just does them to keep me company. In case I get discouraged. It's not that I like eating. I just like a little something every now and then. And that's why I've got hips. I went to this doctor once and he said my hips were just due to little somethings. Some people smoke and I have little somethings. I've tried to smoke but I'm no good. That's my ambition. To be smoky and thin. I don't know if I ever will be. On the whole I think you've got to be more nervy than me. Perhaps I'll be more nervy when I'm older. A lot of people are.

Not many of my relations are hippy like me. Plump all over but not hippy. I've got an awful lot of relations. None of them is what you'd do your nut over. Mostly they're cousins. They don't really care about me and I don't think I really care about them. They'd just be useful if you were an orphan. They're not even real cousins. Most of them are removed in some way. And they come stomping up to you at parties and go on about you being one of their cousins. I bet if you were a lavatory attendant they'd soon forget you were. I shouldn't think they'd even know you. Let alone go about telling everyone you were their cousin.

My mother's hobbies are slimming and dailies. She swears every evening after a huge dinner that she'll go on a diet. Cut down on sherry and everything. She's still on it at breakfast the next morning but by lunch she just feels it's her duty to eat up all the left-overs. She says someone's got to. And if she doesn't no one will. She can't bear to see waste. She says it's because of the war. That's what ruined her figure: not being able to bear waste during the war.

Anyway her other hobby is dailies. She says dailies are more interesting than most people. She has these long conversations with them. About practically everything. She says there's practically nothing a daily doesn't know. One thing she doesn't like much. She doesn't like their operations. She's not much good on operations. Some people are mad on them. They talk about them for hours and hours. And they know all the names of what these

103

operations are called. I don't mind the names, it's when they're actually describing them I don't like it. Once a woman told me about having her bosom removed. It was terrible. Honestly I felt all flat on one side. No, it's true. I had to keep looking down to see I hadn't got a gap. It's terrible when you feel all gappy. Anyhow, that's where my mother gets all the plots for her plays. From all these dailies she talks to.

I'm not keen on operations but I like medicines and pills and glucose. I think it's working in an office that's made me like that. I'm so bored I feel every twinge. So I take all these things to get me through the day. Honestly, it makes the day go much quicker if you take pills and glucose. Also they make something to look at. It's pretty boring just looking at your typewriter or the wall or someone's face. I get this feeling I've got no energy because I yawn so much. I had a boy friend, he was the same. He was a lawyer so he took glucose and pills in between clients. We used to go round chemists together and find new things to take. And he'd ring me up and remind me when to take them. We thought of founding a club for bored glucose-eaters, but he got sent to Manchester so it was no good.

Migo was having quite a boring time too. She was a secretary only she couldn't do shorthand at all. She was the only person I'd ever met who was worse than me. Only her job wasn't as boring as mine, it really wasn't. But she was in love with a footballer, which was pretty awful. Footballers are awful people to be in love with. First of all they never ever love anyone better than their footballs. My cousin told me. She was in love with one too. Then every Saturday they go stomping off and you have to watch them for hours and hours as they kick this football around, then afterwards they drink beer and talk to all these other men who have been kicking it around too. They hardly ever speak to you except during the week. And then they're very tired from having kicked this football around on Saturdays. I don't know what their fascination is really. My cousin says it's probably these shorts they wear on Saturdays. Also they're very muscly, I don't like muscly men, but she does, and she says when they're in these shorts you can see their muscles.

Migo said it was probably their muscles in these shorts too.

She didn't really know for sure, but she thought it probably was. Anyway she used to listen to these very old records wearing his football scarf, and cry about him. It worried me seeing her listening to these records and crying about this footballer. But she said she enjoyed it. She said it did her good to listen to these records; they were really old actually. I mean they were so old you could hardly hear them. In fact, if I had my deaf ear near the gramophone, I couldn't hear them at all.

It took her a long time to get over the footballer. I made her burn his scarf and buy jazz records, but it still wasn't too swoony for her. There really ought to be a purge you could take to get over being in love. Even when you burn a scarf it still doesn't stop you feeling gone inside. It didn't stop Migo. She felt all gone inside every time she even saw a football for heaven's sake.

When she'd got over the footballer, she met her superman. He really is a superman actually. Even my mother thinks he's a superman, and it takes quite a lot for her to think that. No really. She only just thinks my father is a superman. Of course she does think he is, but only just.

Chloë and I were bridesmaids when Migo got married. Chloë was very sad because Migo is younger than her. She hates anyone younger than her getting married. She says it makes her feel unsuccessful. Actually I think Chloë goes in for being sad because she knows it suits her. She has these very large brown eyes and when she looks sad they look marvellous. Now Migo's married Chloë's learning to appreciate beautiful things. No it's true, practically every Saturday she goes about appreciating beautiful things. She says that destiny has not mapped out married life for her. Not for her a superman. And she says it's not just in her nature to marry anyone but a superman. She can't help being a perfectionist. So she's appreciating beautiful things before her eyesight goes. I don't know though. If Migo found a superman I don't see why old Chloë shouldn't. Or anyone else for that matter.

My grandmother says it's unnatural sitting here scribbling. She says I should be out looking for a rich superman instead of being cooped up. I probably am unnatural actually. I mean, what's the point of sitting here talking about all these weeds and drips and things and not doing something about finding a superman? It's just I thought you might like to know. I've probably been as boring as hell. But I just thought I'd have a go at telling you.

Actually you've probably gathered by now a superman takes some finding. They're not things you just come across like that. One friend of mine, she's been looking for one since God was a boy. No luck. Weeds and drips. No superman. She asked me if I thought there was any special place where she might find one. I don't think there is. I don't know, mind you. But I don't think so. I've never been there anyway.

One thing though. I think you can class most men. Supermen, weed, drip, lech. I only met one person you couldn't. He wasn't a superman. He wasn't a weed or a drip. And he wasn't a lech. He was a womanizer but he wasn't a lech. He was only a womanizer when he felt all gone inside. He felt it quite a lot really. What he was, I think, was a vagabond. He was the only person I've ever met who was. A lot of people wander about. But not many are real vagabonds. He was a real vagabond.

I once tried to get two friends of mine to come and be vagabonds with me. But it was no use. They were just no good. All they did was say, what would they do about money? And they couldn't leave their parents. They just had no idea how to begin to be vagabonds. When I was ten I wrote a poem about wanting to be a vagabond. And I ran away from my school to be one. It was a pretty good idea. Only these three other girls I was with didn't want to do anything but go home. It's pretty frustrating,

I can tell you, when you're running away to be a vagabond and you've got all these people just wanting to go home. And it's no good being a vagabond on your own. You must have someone to be poetic with too.

My mother was furious when I ran away from school. She couldn't understand about being a vagabond. She just said if I did it again she'd take me away and send me to a really horrible school. She said it was ungrateful when she'd taken all the trouble to send me to a nice school and all I did was run away. What she was really furious about was this policeman's wife who gave us a huge tea when we got fed up with running away. She couldn't get over us having three boiled eggs each. I said we hadn't had anything to eat all day. And she said I wasn't to answer back. That's what they spend the whole time saying to you when you're young. They ask you something, then when you tell them they say you're answering back and you've given quite enough trouble to everyone without answering back.

When we did get back to school they shut us in our rooms for three days. And this matron walked us in the gardens when all the school was having lunch. They didn't want us spreading evil all over the other girls. She carried a rosary in one hand, this matron, when she was walking us. She said it was protection from the devils in us. She was Irish. And she told us that we'd all burn in hell, and she was praying to save our souls from damnation. She said she didn't think it would do much good, but anyway she was having a go. She said she wasn't one to give up hope, not till the very end.

It was pretty boring sitting in our rooms for three days. But we used to tap on the walls to each other and pass bubble-gum on our toothbrushes through the windows. And one or two of the other girls' parents came down to see them in the parlour. Mine didn't thank goodness. They just wrote me these terribly long, cross letters. Still it was better than having them in the parlour any day.

If I actually told you how I met this real vagabond, you wouldn't believe me. No honestly, you'd just think I was a loon. I met him walking along a road. No, it's true. I was staying with these people in the country. I quite like staying with people in the country. But I get a bit bored after a bit. So often I go for walks by myself and sing and bash hedges with a stick. Because most people you stay with think you're a bit funny if you sing and bash hedges with sticks when they're around.

I was bashing away walking along this road and singing to myself. I can't sing. Well, it's not exactly that I can't sing. Apparently I've got a voice but I just can't sing in tune. When I bumped into this man in front of me. He was just walking along with his hands in his pockets. I just went on singing and bashing away, when he turned off down this drive. It was a very long straight drive with stone gates. You know the kind. And waving trees and deer in the park bit on each side. The kind of drive you die to get on a horse and zoom up with important news.

I stopped when he went down this drive and watched him walking down. It was a very sunny day. Sunny and breezy and he walked in a whistly sort of way. Corney, but you know what I mean. And I felt awfully jealous watching him. I don't know why. I just stood by these stone gates and wished I was walking down this drive in a whistly sort of way too. He was just getting to the top and practically out of sight when I gave a yell. I don't know why I gave that yell either. Actually most marvellous things that you do, you don't know why you do them till you have.

He stopped, when I gave this yell, and turned round. And I ran like anything all the way up this drive. When I reached him he didn't seem surprised to see me at all. That's the best bit about vagabonds, they're never surprised. No honestly. Real vagabonds wouldn't be surprised if you came out of a hole in the ground. I panted a bit when I reached him and he just stood smiling at me. Then I said, did he live there? And he said yes. So I said I wanted to see round. So he said, okay he'd show me. Just like that.

Don't you think that about all really marvellous things? They're *so* corney. When you tell anyone about them afterwards anyhow. I bet Napoleon felt corney when he was telling everyone about retreating from Moscow. Come to think of it, I don't suppose that was marvellous. But you know what I mean. Perhaps that's why they're marvellous. Because they're corney,

corney. And magical and enchanting. That's what that day I spent with the vagabond was like. I spent this whole day wandering round his house with him and walking in his garden. He rang up the people I was staying with and said he was an old friend and could I have lunch with him? For heaven's sake it was like something in a movie.

And his house was like a movie. Beautiful tall rooms and long windows. So you could just step through them and be in the garden. We had lunch in the garden and it was the most beautiful garden you've ever been in. No really. It was all fountains and lawns and shady trees. Like some people think Heaven will be like. It won't half be bad if it is, I can tell you.

I wish I could describe this vagabond without making him sound corney. I can't remember his face. Not all his features anyway. Except he had blue eyes and very white teeth. Though perhaps they only looked white because he had this very brown skin. And he was thin and had a very deep voice. And he was sad. Well, it wasn't that he was droopy or anything. Because he laughed a lot. He just had this terribly sad quality about him. Like a very happy song that catches in your throat.

And he was easy to talk to. Honestly I don't remember word for word what we talked about. But we never stopped. It was just non-stop. If anyone else had been there they'd have been bored stiff. No honestly, they would. I told him things I usually just think and don't tell anyone about. Things most people look really embarrassed if you tell them about them. As if you'd forgotten to put your clothes on or something.

He told me about this woman he'd loved. He really had loved her. No really. And he knew what an awful thing love was. I said I'd never known anything more awful and he agreed. What happened with this woman he loved was, they loved too much. He said they loved so much they destroyed each other. He said that was why he was a womanizer now. And also he got drunk. He knew what all gone inside meant all right, he really did.

I suppose that's why he had this sad feeling about him. Because of having loved too much. I told him about only having been in love once. With this actor. I said most people just said it was infatuation. But he said it sounded like love all right. He said from what I'd told him it didn't sound like infatuation. What he said too was, not to get depressed about it. He said it was much worse never to have known what love was really like than to have loved someone and gone away and been unhappy about it. He said some people never knew what it was like. He said they never would know. Not necessarily just narrow little people either. Often imaginative people who were quite super didn't know what it was like. It just wasn't in them to love like that.

He really could talk, this vagabond. And he could tell you about anything. Like someone people in books are always meeting. Only I'd never met someone like that before. I never have since, come to think of it. He's the only one. All the things you believe in your heart but you're not quite sure you're not a nit believing in them. He made you sure. When he told you about things. Suddenly you knew you were right to believe in them. You knew they weren't corney like most people thought they were. It was only the people that thought them corney that were.

He made you so certain you were right. You could burst. You just thought you must have been mad before not to have been sure. And you were never going to not be sure again. Like when you're happy. You're never going to not be happy again. And you can't remember what you were unhappy about before.

He made you not mind about being *you*. Not mind being someone who cared about corney old abortions. Not mind about having big hips or a pretty funny face. Or anything. Nothing mattered because here was someone who believed, who believed in magic and enchantment. And everything when he was talking was magic and enchantment. Even me. I suddenly knew I was fascinating and magical too. It's pretty marvellous when you sit in an office all day with people minding about whose turn to shut the window when you meet someone who believes in magic. And makes you feel fascinating. Not a plump secretary who can't do shorthand. It's okay to be a plump secretary who can't do shorthand. But it's awful when you *feel* a plump secretary who can't do shorthand.

I never went back to see that vagabond. I've never stayed with those people again either. So he might be dead now for all I know. Or just womanizing round the place. Or perhaps he's making someone else feel fascinating. Perhaps his house has been sold to someone who won't ever want to step through the window into the garden. I don't know. I don't care.

I just know I won't ever go back. You can never make a bigger mistake than going back. The only reason to go back is to try and recapture. And how can you recapture magic? You don't even know what it is for heaven's sake. And how can you get back something when you don't even know what it is. I don't know what it is. I just know I believe in it. And I didn't know what the vagabond's name was. I forgot to ask him. He asked me mine. But I forgot to ask him. It wasn't important anyway.

I don't only believe in magic. I believe in everything corney. I believe that there is a superman. Somewhere. I believe in love. My mother says I'll end up in a two-roomed flat in Hampstead because I do. She says it's the worst thing to believe in. I don't care. I do. And I believe in innocence. You can't stop me. I'm always going to believe in it. Yes I am. Even if I don't find a superman.

I don't think anyone's a failure as long as they're still innocent. Just a little. They may lose everything good in them but as long as they believe just a little in something very small, they're still innocent. To fail is to lose every bit of innocence.

And innocence needn't be beautiful. That's the trouble when you're young, you think there's nothing innocent unless it's beautiful. There are all these millions of things that hurt you because they're not beautiful. No honestly, you go round being practically killed by all these things that are ugly. Lesbians and contraceptives and all that. Then when you're nearly killed, you suddenly laugh. Once you laugh you're all right. If you think, jolly few things laugh. I've got a friend who swears his cat laughs. But it's not what you'd notice. You can't actually hear it when it laughs. And once I was on a bus and there was this big fat woman roaring with laughter. She didn't stop from the time she got on. And do you know all those people on that bus – me too – started laughing. All these frightfully constipated business men and po old housewives and everything. They all began to roar with laughter. Just because of this woman laughing. And they all looked quite different. They stopped looking constipated and po and looked happy. Mostly, though, I should think humans are the only things that laugh. Laughing is what makes humans human.

A lot of people just run away instead though. They don't give themselves time to stop and find something to make them laugh. They run away and start sneering because it's hurting them. Or they run away and just find a swoony spot to hide in so they don't have to see things that hurt. If they really went on looking at something that hurt them they'd realize it was beautiful, and it would probably make them scream with laughter too. Mind you you've got to stick at it.

I'll tell you another corney thing. I'd like to write a love poem to the world. Really I would. Sometimes I love it so much I could die.

Poor tired old world. Poor hungry ill old world. Poor ugly bombed-up old world. Beautiful smiling world. Evil perverted old world. Innocent world. Honestly, even if it blows itself up, it's only because it's so innocent. Poor innocent world, it doesn't know any better.

It's always thinking it's the first to do things. The whole time it's doing things it keeps thinking no one's done it before. It thinks its wars are the worst. Its civilizations the most civilized. Its kings the most important. Its poets the most poetic. Its jokes the funniest. Its queers the queerest. Just because it's so innocent. It keeps forgetting it's all happened before. And when we all go, the next lot of world will think it's the most important bit. And no one will think much about us having thought it all before them. Honestly, you tell me what's more innocent than the world? It's so innocent you can't help loving it.

Coronet Among the Grass

I

I'm beginning this right down the bottom of the page because there's something about beginnings that I don't like. Everyone is always beginning things. My beginnings usually start: 'She sensed something unusual about him that day.' Dot, dot, dot. And then I fall asleep trying to decide what to call myself.

Isabel used to be one of my favourites. I don't know why I really thought Isabel suited me. Worcester never liked Isabel. In fact Isabel got up Worcester's nose. She said she couldn't understand why Isabel had to float everywhere when walking was good enough for everyone else.

Worcester is a friend of mine. She's like a cucumber sandwich – you could never imagine her with crusts. He likes Worcester a lot. In fact he says if he ever *had* to – you know – with anyone else – and then only because he had fallen-into-the-hands-of-the-enemy-and-had-to-save-my-life, he would prefer it with Worcester more than anyone. So it just shows you, because he's been Around, and Known a Few, if you get my meaning. And none of them were what you could call Puddings.

Actually sometimes I get a little choked because every time I pick up *Vogue* or something, there's another of his ex's staring out at me. They're pretty various his ex's. They range from the ones with bra-strap dinner frocks seen enjoying a laugh with Lord Muffin, to the blonde bomb-shell with the big willets and the 'my panties are disposable' smile, who is always seen relaxing with film directors. Well, all I can say is, if that's what she calls relaxing, then heaven knows what really gets her going.

Not that I mind really you understand. It's just that there were so many, that sometimes I wonder how on earth he ended up with me. Not that he did anything about it, ending up with me I mean. It was more like Fate. He had no choice if you see what

115

I mean. He put his card into the computer with 'tall, blonde, 36, 22, 36' written on it, and 'small, brown, 33, 26, 39' came out.

In fact the first time I did meet him he was in a musical, and I thought he was very talented, but far too young. I mean mentally, at the time, I was thinking thirty-five to fortyish, because I was – well, because I was; and he was thinking thirty-six, twenty-two, thirty-sixish, because he always does, so Nothing Happened. Except I did give him a few tips about How to Get On. Actually I was working in a typing pool at the time, and my idea about how to get on was to throw yourself into a room and shout 'you've got to employ me I'm talented', because it once worked for someone I knew. If however you just wanted to be a film star, all you had to do was to open your eyes rather wide every time you went out, and someone was sure to spot you. Actually I didn't tell him that exactly, but pretty nearly, but he wasn't listening because he was waiting for a girl with a really large Pair of Eyes – no really, they were somewhere out to here – well, there.

Anyway millions of years went by and the next time we met I had managed to put on another eighteen pounds in weight, and everything went blank. He was holding a coffee cup and muttering about someone poisoning him, and I was being condescending because I had just written a book and I didn't need men any more. He actually did turn a paler shade of grey and I actually did hear a noise like rushing water, which Worcester says was probably the kettle boiling over, because we were in the kitchen at the time, but I think was Destiny.

Anyway somehow or another we went on from there. Or rather I thought 'I'll show you, old clever drawers', because it's all very well weighing eighteen pounds heavier but it's adding insult to injury when people turn white at the sight of you, I mean I wasn't that fat. Fat, but not That Fat. So every time he tried to ask me out over the next few days I pretended I didn't understand what he meant. Pretending not to understand someone is a question of saying 'sorry, what?' for as long as possible. Of course old Clever Drawers knew better. He just kept saying 'you heard', so in the end I was forced to go to a party with him.

I got in such a sweat before that party. I imagined a huge room filled with chandeliers and bosoms, and I hadn't got a thing to wear, but nothing. It wasn't that I didn't have any bread, because I did, it was just that nothing I liked went further than my shoulders. Anyway the time got nearer and nearer, and I ended up buying something that looked like a blanket, only it was pleated, and that's not something blankets do easily. It didn't really hit me until I was just about to go out of the door – I've never liked looking in mirrors, I prefer pretending, if you know what I mean – but I did look in the mirror and I realized that I couldn't go to a party looking like a cross between Mother Courage and a blanket bath. So I struggled out of it, and put on my old black trousers – très slimming – and a nice pyjama top to cover the rest of me, and off I went, a carefully calculated twenty minutes late, because I wasn't going to show old Clever Drawers that I actually wanted to go to a party with him.

So I arrived. And I saw immediately by the look of his back that he was pretending that he hadn't even noticed that I was late, and what with one thing and another was doing very nicely with a little redhead who was enthusing over his performance. It was really the best thing she'd ever seen in her whole life. Dot, dot, dot.

Of course I didn't take any notice, I just ordered two fingers of red eye and waited by the bar, picking my teeth and jangling my spurs. If there's one thing I despise it's female enthusiasts. I hate them worse than banana yoghurt. Anyway he soon got rid of her and made his way across the pub. I spat out a greeting to him, and noticed he had that glittery look that comes with adulation and a couple of doubles.

I thought he didn't look too keen about taking my trousers to the party, but I reckoned if he wanted me, my trousers came too. I shall pass quickly – as they say in all those books people pretend they've read – I shall pass quickly over the drive through the snow to the glittering party packed with celebrities and casts of thousands, and tell you only that when we arrived I managed to lose him, but not my trousers.

At that time everyone was being very serious if they were Anything to do with Anything, if you know what I mean. It wasn't the thing to look Happy, but it was quite good to have a bright yellow index finger and know the exact number of casualties during the First World War. Things like that are all right, and I must say I usually go along with the crowd, because I'm pretty feeble, but it gets tiring keeping up a northern accent and maintaining a straight face at the same time, so eventually I found myself back sitting next to old Clever Drawers.

It was then that he kissed me, and everything went pink. The funny thing was that it wasn't one of those kisses that people give each other in Art Movies and you're very glad it's not you, if you see what I mean. It was one of those ones that you fling at someone because they've taken you out to dinner, and you hate them but the humanities have to be observed. Very intacta if you get my meaning. And although my dealings with the opposite sex were not what you could call Chatterleyesque, I knew enough to realize that things don't go pink for Nothing. Anyway the fact of the matter was that it wasn't just one of those things. It was The Thing.

Then we ran about in the snow a bit. I won't dwell on it too much because lovers are a big switch off. Particularly when they're leaping about in slow motion wrapping long scarfs round each other, and even worse when they're rolling about rending the air with the tearing of tights and the snapping of suspenders. Anyway after that I went home and pretended to sleep, and he went home and pretended to sleep, and the next morning he took me out to lunch and borrowed a fiver from me to take another girl out.

Actually it wasn't exactly to take another girl out, but to give her the 'darling-we've-had-a-lot-of-fun-and-I-think-you're-gorgeous-but' line. I must say he was quite honest about it, he could be – it was my fiver.

After that the way was clear as it were, and nothing to do but get to know each other as the old joke has it, because the funny thing is when The Thing happens you don't even know each other. I mean it's only after it's happened that you start saying pathetic things like 'how old are you' and 'what's your middle name', because human beings aren't like dogs – one sniff does not reveal all.

Another funny thing is that although you're both saying things like 'my parents live in Bagshot actually', you feel you know anyway, and you're completely unsurprised that he hates trousers with things under the feet, and wasps, and tripe, and bananas, and he *always* has to get down the stairs before it's finished flushing.

And then of course there's the hours spent in saying 'well *I* think it's lovely' which can mean anything from your nose to his crooked finger. Actually it was during one of these 'I think it's lovely' sessions that I did ask him something that I had never asked anyone else. It started when I ventured an opinion, and he said, affectionately, what a load of old cobblers. And I asked him what they were.

Just for a second he honestly couldn't believe it. I mean he really couldn't believe that anyone could reach their majority without knowing what cobblers were. He said hadn't I seen statues and paintings and things? And I said of course I had, and he said well? And I said well what? Statues had nothing to do with it – the point was I'd always heard people saying things, but I kept on forgetting to ask them which bit was which. And by the time I was older I couldn't, in case they laughed. So I just went around pretending I knew anyway. He really did blow his mind. I mean I thought he'd fall under the table. Particularly when he found out what I *thought* they meant.

The funny thing was that it wasn't as if I hadn't read books and things on the subject, but I think I must have missed out a relevant chapter somewhere because there was a gap in my knowledge, if you see what I mean. Worcester was the same. I mean to be absolutely honest we both thought something nice happened, and then you smoked a cigarette, which in certain circumstances could have proved to be a little bit approximate.

Well, after that it became absolute torture because I Knew, he Knew, Worcester Knew, but nobody else wanted to know. It wasn't that Worcester was playing monk to our star-crossed lovers, it was just that back at his pad the last thing chaps were going out with was girls like me, and back at my place it just wasn't on to marry an actor. And I absolutely see both points of view. I mean no right-thinking left-wing actor wants to see his best friends taking up with one of Them. And no thinking parent wants to see their little goldilocks doing the tatty tours with only a couple of sticks of Leichner and an Equity card to keep the wolf from the door.

So once all that's apparent you both have to go about metaphorically killing dragons until everyone realizes how wonderfully wrong they are, and it was an awful sweat. But we happened to think it was worth it.

I must say I wasn't very original. I just plumped for the usual – the Northern accent, the Colin Wilson sweater, and the Royal Court feet, because I couldn't bring myself to take the mothballs out of the Aldermaston duffle. Suitably clothed, I then made sure that every time I went to his flat I ignored the group of vests crouched round the gas fire, and went straight to the kitchen, where I sat frowning and peeling potatoes. Naturally if anyone attempted a greeting of any kind I only acknowledged it after a statutory grunt. Equally I never spoke about anything except with Pain, and I swigged pints in the public bar like there was no tomorrow. Actually, not to be too modest, which is a virtue that doesn't become me, I am quite reasonable at becoming one of the boys.

Not that it's difficult really, as long as you buy your round, punch people in the shoulder by way of greeting, and only open your mouth to pour beer down it, you can get along so nicely that the only time they realize you're different is when you don't go to the jacks with them.

All the time I was doing my Albert Finney however, he was having to do his Little Lord Fauntleroy, and remembering to wear his signet ring on the right finger.

Honestly, what with one thing and another it was a wonder that we ever remembered who we were really. There were all his friends waiting for me to sound like Princess Margaret, and there was all my lot waiting for him to drop his aitches into his gin. Course, part of the trouble was that he could never *find* my father to ask him if it was all right or something. He's one of those very difficult people to make out, my father. It's a knack he developed during the war, and he's never really broken the habit. He can camouflage himself into the drink cupboard better than anyone I know, and staring at walls is positively a hobby with him. So you can come across him in the most unexpected places, or on the other hand if you want to ask him something Important and you go looking for him in expected places, well, you could be there for ever.

In a way I suppose we might still be there now, me doing my Albert Finney and him doing his Princess Margaret, if it hadn't been for Worcester, who had got fed up being the monk and said 'Buy a house and then they can all come and take a drink off you', which as it happened was a very sound piece of advice, because it's funny how quickly people realize how Right you are for each other when you live near by and they're feeling a little thirsty.

So we bought a place, and everyone stopped wishing that he was a lawyer with a private income and I was Iris Murdoch, and came to realize that what must be must be, and he put his signet ring back on the wrong finger and I dropped the Northern accent, and we got married – which was quite the thing in olden days.

2

The first thing I found when I got married was that I had this dreadful problem with his underwear. Somehow everything else would go into the bag wash and come out looking approximately near enough what it had gone in as, but his underwear kept turning itself into floor rags, or falling desperately for the nearest sock and going mauve. It honestly became a real problem. One of those it-or-me situations which can make you wish you'd never said 'I will' in the first place. Or rather you wish you'd said 'I will' to him, but not to his underwear.

Then of course there's this dreadful problem about what to do with all that happiness. There it is sitting all around you, acres and acres of it, and somehow it makes you want to do everything right, even more, if you see what I mean. And as Worcester always says 'never act from good motives' – which is the best bit of advice anyone could give anyone, because if you never act from good motives you'll always be yourself, and that's what that Oracle was always going on about, wasn't it? And anyway you always find people with nervous breakdowns are the ones who keep saying 'I did it for the best', and somehow you know nothing's going to go right until they stop doing it for the best and just do their own thing, and then everyone else will know where they are with them. Well anyway, that's what I think I think.

However at that point I don't think Worcester had actually come out with 'never act from good motives', or if she had, I hadn't been listening because I was too happy, and all that. So not only did I try and act from good motives all the time, but I had a fantastic passion for white – admittedly it had failed to extend itself to his underwear, but in every other way I was perfectly sure that everything should be white. I painted the whole house white, inside and out, including the electric switches and the linoleum. And then I stopped because there was nothing else left to *be* white, but every time I went out I used to dream of miles and miles of white streets, and white pavements, and I wanted everyone to paint their houses white, and I could barely prevent myself from offering to do it for them, because white was my passion and there was nothing else in my own house to get painted.

Then one day when he was out, I woke up and went to the window and realized that the garden – my garden – was not white. There it was sitting below my window completely unwhite. Well that was it. I got to work at once. I painted the walls white, the chairs white, and the tubs white, and then because I didn't like the paving stones to feel left out I painted them white, and the steps, and the drainpipes, and by the time he came home again, the whole garden was completely white, except for the earth which I left brown.

Of course I met him at the door triumphant. I think I even made him shut his eyes first, just to make the surprise even nicer. And I honestly couldn't believe it when he nearly fainted with horror. He said he supposed he was lucky not to find his suits painted white, or his car, or the dog. Actually he said quite a few other things, and by the time he'd finished I'd locked myself in the bathroom, and he was breaking the door down because he thought I was going to commit hara-kiri with the loofah.

Which is another thing about living with someone else. I mean it's not that you don't necessarily like living the same way, but you don't even necessarily like rowing the same way. I mean some people like the swot-you-across-the-ear that'll-give-your-mother-something-to-talk-about routine, and others prefer the I-bet-I-can-break-more-than-you method, which though expensive at least saves you wasting time with words.

As it happens I did not favour either of the above, and nor did he thank goodness. But he's very good with words. He can be incredibly witty at your expense, and I'm so wet I can never think of anything back, so I kept locking myself into things, and he kept thinking I might feel like hurling myself out of things, so a great deal of time was spent with him standing in the road shouting 'don't do it', while I hid under the bed pretending he was nothing to do with me.

In the end we compromised. I stopped shutting myself into things, and he tried not to be so incredibly witty, and one way and another everything was all right. A good deal better than a friend of mine who only came to agree on where to draw the line when he tipped a trayful of spaghetti into her hair and she was forced to go round pretending to be a Sikh because they couldn't get the oil out. Anyway I was very glad he didn't like belting people. Or perhaps he thought I might turn out to be as strong as Worcester, I don't know.

Not that he's a coward you understand. It's just that he's too imaginative. I mean most men once they've had a few and someone starts trying to stick one on them – well they don't *think* about it if you see what I mean – whereas he thinks about it to the *n*th degree, and what it must be like when your teeth are on the floor and they're trying to stick your head back on your shoulders – and it puts him off, and I must say I'm very glad. Particularly when it comes to me.

Actually he hadn't much of a life at school, because he wasn't all beef and muscle, and he liked Beethoven. As far as I can gather if they weren't stringing him up by the toes and calling him names, they were writing him love letters, and then beating him up because he didn't even have the decency to be queer. It's funny how much time is spent beating boys at school. Even when they're old enough to have passed their driving test. I mean if it happened in a factory or something everybody would talk about the Corn Laws and primitive behaviour, but because people pay a lot of money for their sons to be beaten up, well everyone considers it all right, and a privilege and everything. And of course the ones that survive all this lovely treatment grow into the sort of men most women can't stand. You know what I mean – large-bottomed men who prop up the bar, and spill beer all down their Viyella shirts, and call the person they're supposed once to have loved 'old girl'.

Of course I found out all about him and school at the same time that I was finding out how difficult it is to be perfect, particularly when you're married to Clever Drawers. I mean

124

Clever Drawers has perfect taste in clothes. He knows exactly what's in, before it knows itself. I'm not quite so percipient. I'm more likely to have been half an hour at a party before I realize I've put on the coat that the dog had her ghost pregnancy in. He's not like that at all. He's got joosh, and he knows exactly what girls should look like, partcularly me. He thinks I'm inhibited because I won't bare my breasts to have dinner with my grandmother. But what I say is – try *saying* 'breast' in front of my grandmother, let alone show her one. Anyway all the girls he's ever taken out have never been seen in anything except purest cashmere and mink, and even if they had shocking scotches they did at least have crocodile handbags and bottles of Krug tucked into the back of the Aston Martin, and of course Perfect Taste, which is more than could be said of me.

So nothing will do but he must work his little transformation thing with me. The only trouble was that I am not from the same mould as all the Others. I mean What Went Before, is not like What Came After. I don't think he quite realized this – as he took me out to dinner looking like a Michelin man in angora, or urged me on with wild cries as I struggled into leather, and hoped my mother wouldn't see me and make one of her Remarks.

In those days he actually used to take me shopping, I mean he'd come right into the cubicle and sit with me just like a nun at a music lesson. It was awful. Mostly because I could never get into the sort of things that he thought I should get into, and then he'd say things like 'I should take your petticoat off first' or 'I thought you said you were size ten?' as if I'd been deceiving him all those months, and what could you expect if you were tied to someone who couldn't even be Honest about her waist.

Sometimes I did manage to get him to stand outside the cubicle, but in a way it was worse. Because he'd start chatting up all the fantastic birds lolling around outside, and while I was struggling and sweating inside, I could hear him announcing to the world that if only I could throw away my bras all my problems would be solved. Then not content with telling all the world about the current state of my underwear he *would* keep clawing at the cubicle curtain, and shouting for me to come outside where the light was so much better.

Once outside I think I must have Earned my Reward, as Worcester says. Talk about the naffest thing anyone could make you do – parading up and down in front of all those birds who could barely stop themselves from laughing, and half the time were wearing the same things as he'd just made me try on – and he'd keep looking backwards and forwards, and saying 'it looks all right on her', as if I was trying to look horrible on purpose to annoy him. It was terrible. No really.

Anyway he did encourage me to be more Myself. I mean he encouraged me to be more Himself, which encouraged both of us in a kind of way, because then we both felt we were progressing. Although where to was another matter. And in the end I did feel very grateful that he wasn't one of those men that yearn for you to wear black nylon blouses, and patent leather shoes with things like sweeties stuck on the front. I mean he did have Taste, even if my mother couldn't help making Remarks about it.

Actually about this time something else happened to me too. I suddenly discovered that there were such things as rude words, and the best thing about it was that if you said them people realized much faster that you didn't want them to go on doing whatever it was that you'd rather they didn't. If you see what I mean. I mean the trouble with being brought up in England is that they only teach you to say 'please' and 'thank you' and 'I'm terribly sorry', and sometimes it's just not enough. He used to say that if someone ran me over, pinched my money, and stole my car, I'd just say excuse-me, thank-you-very-much-I'm-terribly-sorry. And that doesn't make much of an impression. In fact half the time the only impression it leaves is that they can come back any time and do it again.

Worcester has one point she makes about rude words. She says it just shows you how warped our society is when all the words to do with lovemaking and healthy parts of the body are Rude, whereas if people were normal in any way they'd say really horrible things when they were angry, like 'poisoned tonsils' or 'sewage'.

Anyway be that as it may, another thing happened to me at the same time as all these other things – I started to learn to cook and all that sort of thing. I mean in the old days when I was doing my northern accent and he was doing his Princess Margaret, he used to do all the cooking. And I honestly thought that it was always going to be like that. I really thought I'd always be eating asparagus and telling him how lovely he was.

I soon realized how wrong I'd been. I mean we'd hardly brushed the confetti out of the boot when he was tapping his foot, and telling me he liked his bacon crisp.

Luckily thank heavens I'd had a few cooking lessons, but my range was a little limited. *Blanquette de veau* and *suprême de volaille farcie* are all very well in their way, but knowing how to scramble eggs and make a cup of tea is really rather more useful. Three or four times a week I'd find myself flying down the street in search of new provisions, because whatever it was I was attempting had turned on me, and I had to try and buy some more before he discovered.

I used to dread him going to the dustbins in case he found all the old *fillets mignons*, and avocado ice creams lying around with the muddled eggs, and the dropped scones. It was sweat-making because he only had to pick up an ashtray to empty it, or throw away an old letter and I'd be flying around snatching them from him – honestly I don't know how I didn't have a nervous collapse, what with the dustbin guarding, and the learning how to be a Hostess.

That was even worse than cooking for him. I mean all that cleaning and polishing and making boats out of napkins, all that before you've even begun to ruin a dozen eggs making *sauce béarnaise*, or scorched your fingers trying to glaze the fruit salad. Night after night I used to lie awake hoping that I'd get flu before the Day, or stand by the bathroom window breathing in cold air in an effort to catch pneumonia, so he'd have to call the whole thing off.

The worst time was when we had some Rich to dinner. I mean it's all very well and nice to know rich people when you're going There, but it's awful when they're coming back. I mean for them it's just 'tell the cook we'll be eight' whereas for you it's anything from a nervous breakdown to divorce.

Of course there are the Rich and the rich. I mean there are the

Rich who have only known the Best, and even if they haven't, by now they've forgotten by-mistake-on-purpose what it was like not to be rich, and they don't want to be reminded whatever happens. Then there are the rich – who have always known the best – but bother to think about what it's like to be the Others, if you see what I mean.

What the Rich always say when they ring up is 'listen a boiled egg would be lovely, please don't go to any TROUBLE'. What they really mean is 'we know you're not as rich as us but look we don't MIND'.

However to get back to this dinner thing. So there we were in that sorry situation where you don't particularly like the people, and yet they've asked you to dinner. So now you have to ask them back, which serves you right for going to them in the first place.

And it doesn't help that they gave you perfectly horrible food, but there was a centrepiece of lilies, and napkins so starched that they scratched your knees. I mean it doesn't help because you know, on account of the lilies alone, that you've got to come up with something Good. So after weeks of haggling, you settle on the me-and-you. This time we thought mussels to start with – and then duck, and then pineapple beautifully scooped out and drowned in Kirsch. We got quite over-excited about how lovely it was all going to be.

Anyway there we were in a great state on the Saturday evening, when we realized that, modern fridges being what they were, the little mussels might not last over. So he thought – he has the benefit of a University education – that he would keep the little darlings happy by floating them in buckets of salt water – their natural environment. The only trouble was that neither of us was quite sure how much salt goes to how much water, to make up a standard ocean. So he guessed; and judging by the faces of the other two when they started to eat them, I think it was a good thing that he's only Clever Drawers, and not Head the Ball, because if things had been left to him daffodils would be green.

The point was that the mussels were like lumps of salt. I mean they were so salty they actually burnt the roof of your mouth, and everyone drank the first bottle of Château Wedding Present as if it was Coca-Cola, and tried to pretend it wasn't happening.

Well, that was that of course, except for the fact that by this time I was tiddly, if you know what I mean. What with first-degree burns up my arm from basting the most unbastable fowl that ever took refuge in an oven, and the fact that I knew the caramel in the sauce had lumped itself together and refused to budge, so that it looked like dish water with a toffee floating in it.

Anyway, I managed to wobble backwards and forwards from the dining room ignoring the fact that the peas bounced like gravel round the plates, and that we had so little duck that we had to drape artistic pieces of lettuce round the bones, and make yum-yum noises as if we were at a doll's tea party.

The pudding course would have been all right, if it hadn't been for the fact that I dropped it. Dropping pineapples doesn't improve them. In fact if you drop a pineapple it tends to resent it, it tends to sit about the carpet in small yellow lumps defying you to pick it up. And even when you do manage to grasp it it seems to insist on bringing a lot of inedible fluff with it.

When he found me in a corner trying to get the fluff off the pineapple, he said: 'Along alone atlast the riverrun', which is a very Joycean reaction. And then he said a great deal more. It's pretty impressive to know that you're living with someone who has Joycean reactions, but it doesn't help you to get fluff off pineapple.

Bending down trying to get fluff off pineapple isn't the sort of thing you plan for dinner parties. I mean when you're planning what you're going to wear and all the witty things you're going to say, you don't usually include crawling about carpets getting fluff off pineapples. Just as you don't expect to have mussels like lumps of salt, and corked wine. And it's no good telling yourself that worse things have happened to friends of yours, and remembering that someone, somewhere once dropped something worse, because they're not here. Only you are here, and you've still got another ten pieces of pineapple to go.

By the time I got back to the dining room, Clever Drawers was getting the Big Red Mouth. The Big Red Mouth is something you learn to recognize. It manifests itself when people are talking about skiing, which you don't do, or hunting, which you don't like. It says: 'Would you like to go upstairs for coffee now?', only it sounds like: 'Widge joo like to go 'stairs fer coffee no?' It is usually a result of me saying 'Don't argue.' I always say 'Don't argue' about everything. I hate people shouting, it's one of my main drawbacks. Besides that, I'm a devout moral coward. I've never owned up to anything in my life. I don't believe in standing up for things, only getting round them. And as for someone pulling all your toenails out – I mean you might need them.

Of course halfway through coffee, when I had calmed down, I realized that not only were we not in the same league as these people, we weren't even on the same planet. I mean it's all very well when you're over at their place swigging the Napoleon Brandy and making 'How now brown cow' noises. But when they're back with you it's not the same. You realize that because your coffee is not served by a maid they feel terribly sorry for you. You realize that they are trying to make conversation *at your level*. They're bending down to your eye-level grill trying to imagine what it must be like to be you, and hoping they won't get fat in their eyes. And they will keep saying 'Are you *sure* I can't help you with the washing-up?', as if they're going to have a sleepless night thinking of you with your hands plunged in hot soapy water and them not there to help you. Exclamation mark, exclamation mark.

Actually, you had to realize that they were trying their best. I mean, in trying to come down to our level they made a big effort to brighten up their conversation, make it more King's Road, and that sort of thing. They said 'yer actual' about everything, and referred to their 'mates', and having 'a good nosh'. And they talked about pot and grass, and turning on and switching off, and tuning in and dropping out, and all before you could stop them to explain that you weren't like that. I mean according to their dictionary, if you weren't rich and drinking Napoleon Brandy all the time, then you absolutely had to be With It, otherwise they wouldn't be around to know you. It's very difficult to stop and explain that you aren't Right Up There with the After-Eight Society and all that bit – exclamation mark – to people who are convinced that you are.

'We're totally exhausted,' the Rich Man yawned. 'We were up all last night smoking pot.'

It's difficult to know what to say to people making remarks like that. I find myself staring at my feet, and realizing that I've got a mole on my left wrist when people make remarks like that. I mean what are you meant to say? 'Gosh how super?' Or, 'I believe it's groovier with self-raising flour'? Remarks like that pose severe social questions. If you say to people 'I had a double gin last night', you can expect them to think you've got a pretty average outlook. Anyone who told you they were up all night drinking gin would not get ten for being witty and vivacious. But somehow it seems to be different with grass. Grass seems to demand a sort of between one thing and another reaction, neither to coo-coo nor to yum-yum. Somewhere between the two, finely judged and well-put. I said 'Good Heavens' and got a look from the Big Red Mouth, who started to talk earnestly and incomprehensibly about Ethics.

Meanwhile, she was intent on trying to find out How Much I had Earned. This is what people are interested in more than anything else when you've written a book, but they never ask you properly. They never come right out with it, and say 'How much did you earn?' They kind of swim all around it, half wanting to know, and half wanting not to – in case they don't like your reply.

And if you tell them, I mean if you really just cut off their question and tell them, they hate it – and you, and they give you funny looks as if they now have you really Summed Up. You're one of those people who go round telling everyone how much you've Earned, you're one of those awful people who go round Boasting about what you're coining. And once you've told them the answer to what they've been asking, they don't want to know you any more. Telling people how much you've earned is like mentioning Titles. Mentioning Titles is very bad news. If you mention Title to someone they curl up. If you say 'Marchioness', even quite informally in conversation, people will move away from you very fast, and point you out as being one of Those people. You can mention fame all right though. You can say anything you want about fame. You stand in a corner and rattle off the names of all the famous people you have ever met, and people will find you witty and interesting and the life and soul, and full of whey-hey-hey. Just like you can tell people you earned a lot of money – but not How Much.

I suppose it was because I said exactly How Much that she decided to switch on and turn round and drop out, and so did he. They asked Big Red Mouth Clever Drawers if he minded, but since he had started to disappear under the coffee table, his reply was not altogether audible, at least not to mortal ears. It was the first time I'd ever seen anyone rolling a joint of grass. It took them a long time, and a lot of spreading out of handker-chiefs, and much licking of cigarette papers. And then they kept passing it between them and giggling, finally ending up crouched round a radiator cap on a radiator, saying how mind-blowing it was.

So anyway, after a few 'Man–it's beautiful!'s, and 'Wow*ee*'s, and other well-known clichés, they went home and we did the washing up. And Clever Drawers said: 'Well I thought that went off all right' about fifteen times. He's very optimistic like that. No really. He even thought the pineapple was lovely.

3

I'll tell you one thing though, I certainly wasn't really pulled together when I had a success. Some people by the time they get to twenty are pretty well in control. I wasn't – I was pretty well out of control. Of course no one quite believes you. No one quite believes that anyone can be that stupid, and looking in the rear-view mirror I can hardly believe it myself, but it was true.

Part of the trouble was that I was discovered. I mean I'd been there all the time, but suddenly someone decided I hadn't, and shouted 'you're discovered', so I was. Of course everyone, including you, has always *wanted* to be discovered. I mean everyone's sat around dreaming about having close-ups of their nostrils in magazines, and going to premières in their nighties, but when it happens, you don't want to know.

Well at least you don't think you do, just as you don't really think you want the money. And although you can't remember all those witty replies you had ready for the John Freeman interview, you can remember thinking when you finally finished your masterpiece that no amount of money in the world would make you sell it. I mean other people might want to go around baring their souls for money, but you had discovered that the crock of gold at the end of the rainbow was a piece of paper and a pencil.

Not surprisingly, no one takes the slightest bit of notice of you. There you are muttering about just needing a long robe and a pair of sandals, and there are all of them saying 'well why did you write it then?' because they are labouring under the illusion that people write books for other people to read, whereas you know that people write books At First for other people to read, but then they don't want them to. It's what Clever Drawers calls a dichotomy.

To go back to the start, I wrote this book when I was a typist, because I thought there had to be something more to life. Being a twit I didn't realize that if I wanted to be a Happy Typist, I couldn't also be a Budding Genius, mostly because if you want to get on in an office you must be indistinguishable, if not invisible. If however you do not do everything to be indistinguishable you will turn out to be very bad news, and have no one to blame but yourself.

It doesn't do just to be indistinguishable looking, you have also to do indistinguishable things – like knitting and talking about each other, and spending your lunch hour eating mushroom omelette. If you don't do these things you are not one of Les Girls, and not to be one of Les Girls can make things pretty uncomfortable, and as for writing in your lunch hour – well you might as well do the strip in the canteen as far as they're concerned.

At first you don't quite realize just what a joke you've become, and then you know because you find out that they read bits out of your book aloud when you're not in the room – and say 'had it published then?' when you're going off for lunch, and sometimes just for a few seconds you feel like murdering someone, but you don't, you just think 'you wait' – and that goes for all of them.

If I'd known Worcester then she'd probably have said 'what can you expect?', or 'very naughty of them', but I didn't. I just got used to everyone talking every time I went out of the room, and then stopping when I came back, and not having any carbon paper when you'd run out, and every time you started a conversation being too busy to listen.

Then one day someone really does want to buy what you've written, but really, and you hop skip and jump all the way to the same old bus stop, and the 'you wait' that you've been saving up inside you is exploding, and you get to the middle of the room, and the typewriter covers are being taken off and the knitting unravelled, and you feel like the cowboy with the white hat in the pictures who's spent the whole two hours tracking the villain, and at last got him up against the wall. 'EUREKA' would be appropriate. Or one of those truth-is-stranger-than-fiction drunken speeches.

But it doesn't quite come out like that. I mean after all those hours spent visualizing what you'll say, somehow the words do not flow as smoothly as when you used to dream about it in your bath. Coming out with 'I say, I've sold my book,' isn't as easy as it sounds. Particularly when everyone else is intent on wondering whether or not to have a doughnut with their coffee. Inevitably it all comes out wrong, and at the end of the day you go home knowing why the cowboy never does feel like smashing the villain when he catches up with him. Somehow, when it comes to it, it's just not something you want to do any more.

Of course what I didn't know was that the same goes for having a success. I mean I'd always imagined that success meant flowers and tributes, and pretending not to notice the admiration lurking at the back of people's eyes, and a sort of general smoothness of existence like old brandy. I never expected it to be lowering – but then I was extraordinarily stupid. Ask Clever Drawers, he said I was like the eskimos before they discovered alcohol.

For one thing I never stopped crying. First of all I cried because I had to give the manuscript to the person who wanted to publish it. Then I cried because the publishers wanted to give me some money, and although I wanted to leave the typing pool I realized that in taking the money I was admitting that a robe and sandals was not quite enough, so I cried even more – and cashed the cheque.

Then I cried every time someone took me out for a business lunch, because I thought nothing nice was ever going to happen again. I cried in all the top restaurants. Sometimes I just held the menus in front of me, and sometimes I hid behind the roller towels in the cloakrooms, and sometimes tears dripped down my nose into my *café filtré* without anyone noticing at all.

The thing was I had this idea that my way to the stars was now blocked. I mean I didn't realize that it would all be over in a second – I really thought that that was what the rest of my life would be – munching lobster thermidor and watching people dribbling cream down their chins, which is all very well if you like that sort of thing, but I didn't. Of course if I'd had the brains to ask somebody they could have told me, but being sadly lacking in that direction, I didn't, I went on thinking that when I cashed that cheque I bit on the apple of destruction. Nothing was going to be the same again, and I would grow a double chin and feel peeved if the doorman didn't remember my name.

Besides this tendency to blub, I behaved fairly well. I did exactly what I was told, and I didn't do anything I shouldn't – like talk to the photographers hanging from the trees outside the bathroom – or tell fat columnists exactly what they could do with their offers to share their beds. Anyway I knew I had to shut up, because I had no one but myself to blame. A question of paying your way and taking your chance.

The problem was these funny ideas that I had about being a success and getting discovered. I mean I really believed all those books that make success sound like a toy department, with everyone inside rushing about in tinsel dresses and occasionally all of us from hardware, and haberdashery, being allowed to have a peep. I actually thought that when I gave up the idea of only owning a robe and sandals, that it was in favour of a bit of Whoopee, and Ho Hum Charlie. I thought people would appear nicer, and make their well-bred sneers behind a veneer of urbanity, and while naturally I would Not Be Fooled – I could at the same time probably admit to enjoying myself.

The point was that no book I had ever read told you how rude success is – which is extraordinary because, far from people hiding their sneers beneath their urbanity, they get right up close to you, so you can see their sneers better. And while I had read once of people spitting all over Noël Coward's evening dress, it was at least because they hadn't liked the play. I mean they had actually seen it, and then spat. Whereas as far as I could see nowadays people spat first, before they'd even read what you'd written.

I used to spend hours trying to work out clever replies to people, but I was a non-starter every time. No matter how much preparation I had done all those 'the price of everything and the value of nothing' epithets would fly out of my grapefruit size brain, and I would say something really witty and clever like 'you are horrible'.

It wasn't just the smart replies I tried to work out either, I used to labour endlessly over my props. I mean at a time when books about prison visiting were in fashion, it didn't take much to realize that 'Memoirs of an Upper Class Typist' could be bad news as far as interviewers and people went, so my props were something to cling to. Not just hip flasks and worry beads, but my hair as well, which I tried to encourage to grow right over my face so the Enemy couldn't see me going a paler shade of grey.

I must say I failed dismally all the time. The Enemy didn't have to bother to see my face, they could hear my teeth chattering all the way from the car park. And somehow a swig at the hip flask wasn't quite enough when you heard someone say 'God Not Her' as you walked in, and young men in television studios with ear phones and sorbo rubber jackets, stuffed hankies in their mouths every time you said something, or said 'people like you', because it wasn't often you got a real live Upper Class Twit within firing distance.

Sometimes I got so tired of trying to prove that I wasn't everything they wanted me to be, that I contemplated removing the mothballs from the Aldermaston Duffle, but there really wasn't much point. They had polished up their rudes for weeks, and not even the smell of mothballs from the Aldermaston Duffle would have deprived them of their chance.

Still the money was lovely, and in the end that's all I used to think about. Every time a journalist asked me whether I'd slept with Royalty, or been to bed with my agent, I just used to close my eyes and see these lovely blue five pound notes floating by. It was sort of capitalist's yoga, if you get my meaning. And however irritable you feel (which you shouldn't because you got yourself into it – no one else) somehow the thought of how much you're earning makes you feel very benign. A long way from the robe and sandals days.

My father felt far from benign. I mean it was his gin all these people were drinking. It didn't matter what time they arrived they'd hardly put their cameras down, when they somehow managed to get their Andy Pandy's round a drink. And not happy with swigging his alcohol they used to make him pose for photographs, or ask him didn't he wish he'd written my book?

Or even was it true that he had? I tell you once or twice it was a good thing those people were talking to a Patient Man, because he's got a lot of muscle on him my father, once you find him that is.

One quite interesting thing though, and that is the discovery of just how little you really do know about what goes on. You see I thought I knew a bit, because I was so steeped in old movie stars' biographies, but I never realized to what lengths people went to try and earn five guineas from a gossip column. It's extraordinary really, because they spend much more than they could hope to get back – bribing people and hiring tape recorders, and hiding in other people's flats with telephoto lenses. If that's what they do when you write a book, heaven knows what it must be like if you're Really Somebody.

Anyway Clever Drawers was far from benign about everything. In fact, by and large, he didn't help at all. He was always fearing the worst. And he kept thinking he should be there, and hiding himself behind trees and standard lamps. It didn't matter how old or tired the reporters were, he'd hardly gone to bed when he'd be up again, and back round at my house. Nothing would convince him that all foreigners weren't rapists. And if he wasn't allowed in the house he would sit outside in his car glaring at the front door and playing the radio so loud that some poor chap who was in the middle of saying 'êtes-vous part of Swinging London?' wouldn't wait for an answer, but would fly back to his paper convinced that 'le boom boom' originated chez me.

Of course there are various things which are *de rigueur* when you're going around being successful. Like spending the whole time getting on and off aeroplanes wearing dark glasses and carrying teddy bears.

Refusing to speak to people is another very successful thing to do. As soon as people think you're trying not to tell them something they get riveted. Instead of lashing out on shampoo all you need to do is to buy the Complete Airport Arrival Kit – Hat, dark glasses, and a twist of pot in the vanity case – with an arrow so customs don't forget to arrest you. And then you refuse to speak, thereby ensuring a front page photograph with the caption 'NOTHING TO SAY'.

Still although I kept having to arrive at airports I didn't have any dark glasses, or floppy hats, and I didn't have any cool either. Some travellers have a lot of cool. The ones I always envy are the people who sidle into the V.I.P. lounge wearing all in one towelling suits, and on a flight to Bangkok carry only a bar of chocolate and a copy of the *Formosa Times*.

I never stopped being Uncle Dick. Nice people had only to give me flowers, or ask for my passport, and an overwhelming urge to be unwell would come over me. Then I'd emerge from the cloaks pretending I hadn't been – because I have this very English thing about pretending things aren't happening.

Anyway quite apart from being Uncle Dick, and not having any cool, I also didn't like packing. Clever Drawers said he once unpacked two of my suitcases, and found a pair of tights in one and a sponge bag in the other. Of course he never helped. He was always standing around fearing the worst. And just as you had your foot on the runway he would murmur 'You see I don't understand how they stay Up' – which does nothing to heighten your cool, or anything else for that matter.

Even if I remembered my dark glasses and my floppy hat, I'd forget my vaccination certificate. It's very difficult to keep up the incognito smile when a customs officer is crawling round your legs trying to find a scar.

Still, staying on your own in hotels can be very good news, because it allows you to polish up your character parts – particularly at breakfast because somehow people notice each other more at breakfast, and you get better opportunities for making an entrance.

I must say I haven't got a very large repertoire, nor a very original one, although 'Garbo Grand Hotel' did become one of my favourites. The figure was a bit of a drawback, because when I'm attempting the lissome walk it's more inclined to be a Neapolitan sway, but if you get the hat at the right angle, and you've been up late enough to eradicate a bit of the Public School and added a little bass – it can pass muster.

The 'Mad Butterfly' can also be quite good. Smudge the eye make-up a little, radiate spring morning smiles, make sure you're sitting at a table for two, and tell the waiter 'He Won't be Down'

– and before long the whole dining room will be aware that you are having an affair with a bastard. Part of the reason they know this is because you're so nice he has to be.

Besides hotels and aeroplanes, success means having a lot of interviews. These are very disappointing compared to what you imagined when you were in your bath. I mean in your bath you imagine yourself being asked interesting difficult questions, to which you will make interesting difficult replies, and you see yourself effervescing and epigramming and people's pencils flying over their notebooks, but it's not like that at all.

I suppose it was something to do with the fact that the person being interviewed was me, because all I ever got asked was where I went to school, how old I was, and how long it took me to write my book. Actually I've never understood why how long something takes has anything to do with anything, but still it's very difficult to be witty about your age, your school, and how long you took to write something. Well, it is if you're me.

Sometimes I got a bit fed up, and told them what they wanted to know, rather than the truth, which wasn't what they wanted to know – and anyway was a bit tedious.

I told them I was brought up on a crumbling estate by an old and faithful nanny. And my father was a well-known eccentric who was always in the library while my mother rode daily to hounds. My brother was a guards officer who gambled heavily, and my grandmother had retired to Monte with the family jewels. Now I was rich from my book which had Rocked Society – I was going to restore the old family home, give my nanny a new hot water bottle, and put up a monument to pony.

They liked that much better, and you couldn't blame them. I mean you have to make pretty patterns if you're putting someone into print.

Of course Clever Drawers used to do his nut, in between trying to keep his signet ring on the right finger. He kept on not seeing the connection between posing in your nightie for *Life* magazine, and having written a book. I mean he still had these old fashioned ideas that authors were respectable people who lived at Honeysuckle Cottage and grew their own cabbage. I could see his point of view, but it's easier to see someone's point of view than it is to do something about it.

There are certain insuperable problems when being confronted with eager photographers, most of them being the eager photographers. It doesn't matter how many times you tell yourself the very next time they turn up you will give them five minutes, a cup of instant and the boot, when they finally appear smiling on your doorstep, puffing and panting under the burden of their equipment, somehow you always find yourself helping with the lights and Sympathizing. As soon as you find yourself Sympathizing you've had it.

I mean there's the poor chap Only Doing His Job, and he's probably got a wife and children, and just one more picture won't do any harm. And then he's come all the way from Stilton-under-Lyme, and it seems churlish to refuse just to pop on your nightie, and let him take a picture of you At Work.

Mind you that was another thing Clever Drawers couldn't understand. He said why couldn't I work in clothes like everyone else. I said because I'd always been a night worker. He said night workers on the Underground didn't work in nighties, which I had to admit was true, so what was so special about me I had to go leaping into a nightie every time I wanted to work?

It's difficult to think of an answer to that sort of thing. I mean you don't want to say you're Special, because that's asking for quite a few ribald comments, and ribald comments are the sort of thing that can confuse someone to whom answers do not come easily. Finally I said, hopefully, that I only felt inspired when I was in my nightie, at which he looked very dark, and muttered about making myself a laughing stock.

Anyway the good thing was that when it all stopped and it was Dear Diary – Got Up – No Interviews – Went to Bed, at least I could say I'd done it. Not that it qualifies you for a job mind you. I mean it's not a patch on shorthand and typing like that. Still I learnt one or two things. Like money is nicer than fame, and taking taxis lessens your power of observation. It could have been worse.

And then just for a minute I thought I was going to miss it. I don't know, maybe it was just a panic, but once just for a second when I was passing one of those rich restaurants at lunchtime I thought I wouldn't be averse to glancing at the cake trolley one more time. Or even mulling over a truffle or two at someone else's expense.

Perhaps it was something to do with the fact that there was a smell of garlic wafting through from the basement, or perhaps I had one of my cream slice days on. One of those days when you try hard to stare at thin clothes, and thin girls, and talk to yourself long and hard about face brighteners, but all you can see is cream slices. And girls behind cosmetic counters smile pearly smiles, but you only see the pearly glow of the cream, and their lipsticks pink and glowing are reminiscent only of that dearer pink by far – raspberry jam.

It's start again time. It's Real Life once more. Pretending to write as you count the raindrops on the window, and struggle to suppress the urge for suet roll. Frowning intensely when asked What You're Doing Now?

That is the one great thing that success can do for you – it can take the achievement out of life. It can make you sit about for months afterwards incapable of action. You keep trying to jump out at yourself shouting 'care, damn you, care', but nothing happens. You just keep falling asleep. Or spend hours writing out your name dozens of times to make sure you're still there. The thing is success does change you. It makes you want to fall asleep.

4

Something I never thought I'd become, and that's a wife. Even just thinking that word sends shivers down my spine. I suppose it's because wives are always depicted as people in flowered aprons with washing powder on their minds. I mean I know it's the highest compliment someone can pay you, but somehow that's not how it feels.

What's so strange is that you don't think of yourself as a wife. So okay you've got married, but that doesn't mean to say that you've automatically become a wife – you think. That is until you go out one evening and a blonde in a red maxi flutters her false eyelashes at you, and says 'so *you're* his wife' as if you were a piece of flocked wall-paper. And you're busy looking behind you wondering who they're talking to, and you suddenly realize they mean YOU. You're the person their tone of voice has turned into a pudding. And then they say 'you don't mind if I BORROW him do you?' as if he was an L.P. or something, and off goes old Clever Drawers smirking slightly as if he's just being polite, and you're left beside the vol-au-vents with a draught whistling down your backless, and your eyelashes making waves.

Actually once left beside the vol-au-vents you get a bit uncomfortable, remembering how many husbands you've chatted up, before you became a wife yourself. I mean you can't blame other girls for what you've done yourself. Mind you half the time you don't realize it. I mean half the time you think you're being bright and gay, and sparkling like all get-out, and then you catch someone's eye and they're having apoplexy in the corner, and you realize that they think you're devouring their husband. And all the time you thought you were just making conversazione.

Actually one of the most irritating things that can happen to you is to be treated by some people's wives as if you were a former scarlet girl friend, when all the time their husbands are the sort of men that were enough to make you shout, but the next minute the maggie that did marry him is giving you the big 'I know all about you' look, and it occurs to you that for want of something better to talk about hairy old Angus has blown your one visit to the cinema together into the 'A to Z of Love'.

However parties viewed from behind the vol-au-vents are not a wow, even if you know you had it coming to you. I mean you've spent hours and hours sticking your eyelashes on, and trying to resist Clever Drawers' attempts to make you up, and pulling dresses on and off you in the excitement of being asked out and now you're left having a tête-à-tête with the vol-au-vents.

Actually I often think that's the best thing about parties – the before bit. The getting dressed and 'is this all right?' bit. And Clever Drawers saying 'let me do your eyes for you', and making you look like a reject extra.

Well, at least that's usually the bit I enjoy most, because once I get there I can never see anyone as nice as Clever Drawers to talk to, and even if there is, I've only just got to begin holding forth, and Puff the Magic Dragon is beside me announcing that we have to go home, and telling me how tired I look. Not that he's ever jealous you understand – he just feels that I need an early night. At Once.

So there you are full of Eastern promise, and you get to thinking that before you became a wife you used to have quite a good time at parties, but now you're a wife and not interested in passing your telephone number round, you're not only treated like a pudding, you most likely *are* one. It's very distressing.

Mind you you're not the only one it happens to. It happens to lots of other people too. It's not only the girls' fault either, I mean some men can't wait to rip off your hair piece, and fling you the rubber gloves. Sometimes it is the girl though.

I had a friend once, called Gloria, who was just too delicious for words, and it happened to her of all people. It was incredible because Gloria was Gloria. And she was the last person you'd think it could happen to. I mean she smelt of Miss Dior when we were all still playing doctors and nurses, and by the time we smelt of Miss Dior, she was back playing doctors and nurses. Gloria was ADVANCED, and she wanted people to love her for herself at a time when we would have given all our 'O' levels for someone to love us for our bodies.

Anyway she got married and went to live in the South of France. Every day when I got on the bus to go to the typing pool I used to think of Gloria sitting in the South of France among all that mimosa, and I used to imagine her toying with a freshly caught trout, or tossing a *Salade Niçoise*, and that thought kept me going. I mean Gloria was a princess, and princesses should live in the South of France with the mimosa and toss *Salade Niçoise*.

Little did I know that the only *Salade Niçoise* Gloria was making was of her life. She'd married one of those males who are always described as International Lawyers, when they're really Something Dropped Off A Lorry merchants. And they have hair that curls up from their collars, and everyone's mother is always saying how *charming* they are. Anyway I suppose it was too easy for Gloria to just take his cheque book and relax, she had to start trying to use her brains. I believe she had some crazy idea that the Something Dropped Off A Lorry merchant had married her for herself alone – the inner sparkle he saw gleaming beneath the gold of her tan. So she let her unnatural blonde grow out, and she took up reading, and when they moved back to London she started having babies and wearing Dr Scholl sandals, and every time you had tea with her she kept saying 'I haven't used make-up for years', as if it contained nicotine.

I couldn't believe how awful she looked, and of course the next thing that happened was that she discovered old Curly Locks in the Wendy House playing au pairs and masters, and that was that. Nothing to do but wear bedroom slippers all day long and open a restaurant in Cornwall.

Of course where Gloria went wrong was to try and use her brains, because she hadn't any. And the reason she tried to use her brains was that she thought being a wife meant being different from being a blonde. She really thought that once you were married you had to take life seriously and stop worrying about whether you were delicious any more. I mean that's how wrong people can get about being a wife.

Still some girls don't get it wrong. They really do go on trying to be delicious, until they find that it takes money to be lovely, and he isn't giving them any. Honestly, it's incredible, some men are so mean you just wouldn't believe it. They spend the whole time saying 'but I gave you fifty pence yesterday' and wondering why she's looking down in the mouth. And they expect her to cook brain stew and have babies in the front room, and still be up in the morning to bring them a cup of tea. It can be pretty disillusioning when you go to someone's wedding and they're as pretty as a bunch of flowers, and the next minute they're sitting in your kitchen wearing flat shoes, and pinching all your cigarettes.

It's this funny thing that comes over men as soon as they're married, they keep thinking you're their mother. Very often you don't look in the least bit like their mothers, at least not to begin with, but if they have their way, after a few hundred years of washing out their socks, no one will know the difference.

Mind you the sort of woman who gets up my nostrils is the one who spends the whole time verbally knocking out her pipe on her shoe and as soon as she gets pregnant sits around saying 'I don't know what I'll do if it's a Girl', as if girls are the next best thing to ptomaine poisoning. And that seems to be the crux of the matter, if you know what I mean. Women who spend the whole time waving the Female Flag can't wait to bring up their sons to think they're the bee's knees, and drive some other woman round the proverbial.

Still that's neither here nor there really, because any amount of Female Liberation doesn't get you out from behind the vol-au-vents. But you do have time to start wondering whether Clever Drawers knew what he was doing when he bought you the velvet shorts and the elfin boots. And the other thing you wonder about is how some women DARE – I mean to say they don't mind what they do, so long as it's quite plain what they'd like to do.

That's the other thing you don't quite realize when you first become a wife – that there's this very subtle kink in some women's make-up – they just don't want to know about what they can get. In fact what they can get is très boring. I didn't catch on to this for ages. I mean I'd waddle happily into parties and drift away from Clever Drawers – only to discover hours later on the way home that someone had nearly raped him in the sauna.

Just at first I used to think it would be pretty difficult to rape Clever Drawers, because he's very straight and, unlike nowadays, the bloom had not worn off me; and then I suddenly realized that he was extremely vulnerable because of his stomach. I mean he has a stomach like a vegetable sieve, and it only has to come in contact with a little tiny gin and tonic and he's mistaking the hat stand for his mother.

Naturally you can't blame a person for their stomach, you just have to understand what the routine is, particularly when it's a very large party and there are lots of waiters swooping about, and he keeps reaching absent-mindedly for another one. And then when you go and collect him, you find him in a corner with his nose in the Foreign Secretary's ear shouting about Suez.

The first time I realized what an effect gin could have on a person was when I found him in the hall telling the waiters how beautiful I was. It was awful, because I had to keep pretending that I wasn't noticing, and there were a whole lot of hooray henrys laughing at him. I could have pushed their faces in, but I didn't, I just dragged him over my shoulder and staggered out to the car.

Even getting him into the car was difficult because people seem to go all floppy when they're drunk, as it were. I mean you keep stuffing one bit in, and then another bit falls out. Then once we were home I nearly expired because our new neighbour was saying good night to someone on her doorstep, and waving good evening to us at the same time. And I kept calling good evening back, but she didn't budge, and she didn't budge. Honestly I must have called good evening seventeen times, but she still stood there. So in the end I just opened the car door, and he spilt into the road like a can of beans. I'm sure she thought he was an alcoholic.

Actually Clever Drawers does have a habit of having to be

rescued at parties. Even at dinner it's not safe to leave him too long. Once I wondered why he kept waving to me, and trying to cut his steak with a fork, and it turned out that the girl sitting next to him was trying to undo his trousers. Another lady wrote 'meet me in the pantry' in lipstick across his napkin during the *hors d'œuvres* for heaven's sake. I mean she couldn't even wait for mains, she had to get in there straightaway.

He says that it's his sympathetic face that attracts certain elements. He says women want to talk to him, tell him all their troubles, and that sort of thing. But I don't see why you have to take a man's trousers off in order to tell him your troubles; but there you are, I suppose some women are so boring it's the only way they can get a man to listen to them.

As it happens I don't mind any of that, but I get pretty sticky if people push it too far. Particularly the ones who think the best way to get to know him is through you, and they're forever sitting round your kitchen asking for recipes and then giving him the big come-on when you're Hoovering. I suppose it's narrow minded, but they really get up my nostrils. I'd much rather the straightforward 'come up and see me sometime' type, I mean at least you know where you are, whereas the other lot as soon as your back's turned they're calling round and asking him to help them with their golf swing. Or else they write him long letters to say how much they enjoyed working with him, and sign themselves hoping to see him in the VERY NEAR future.

Still Worcester always says if you marry an actor you've got to expect it. But what you expect is having to watch him having all his clothes ripped off, and people kissing him on screen and that sort of thing, you don't expect this constant nibbling that some women go in for. They just can't keep themselves to themselves.

It's not just actresses either. Some girls may not enclose photographs of themselves relaxing in their father's garden at Hendon, but they write him long postcards saying how they're *dying* to meet *me*, and wouldn't it be fun to talk over old times, and then when you go round they sit there all evening playing out the old line about what fun it was when they were rushing about in their old cars, and wrapping college scarfs round everything. Not con-

tent with that they have to keep turning round to you and
saying 'you would have *loved* it' or 'it would have done you so
much *good*'.

And then they keep on saying 'how's old Butch?' And everyone's always described as having a 'ding dong' or a 'bang', which
makes me start going cross-eyed thinking of all those softies
camping around while I was being a typist. And then if you say
ONE thing about University education they all leap down your
throat and start singing snatches from the University lampoon –
or worse still make you listen to tapes of shows with everyone
playing old men and char ladies. It's enough to put you off the
intelligentsia for ever. Still I'm just jealous really – just because I didn't have any brains. The way I go on about having
worked man and boy since I was sixteen you'd think it was a
virtue to be stupid.

That's not the only jealousy I suffer from either. I'm always
being jealous in my mind, particularly when I'm ironing. I
imagine Clever Drawers coming home and being Honest with
me. I see him telling me all about this blonde in a red maxi that
he's irresistibly drawn to, and he hopes I'll forgive him.

Or else he's just completed a film and when he comes back I
feel there's something Different about him, and then one evening
he Blurts Out all about the time he was on the beach, and suddenly his and this girl's bodies melted into one. I'm usually quite
forgiving with that one, because he was so far away in a hot
country.

It isn't always easy though. Not when he goes and falls completely in love with someone else. Not when he goes on like you,
and *admiring* you for being a wonderful wife, but the Big Thing
has turned up and the call of the wild must be answered. That
isn't easy at all.

I always see myself saying things like 'I'll always put you first
my love', and waving from the front doorstep, when in reality
I'd probably crash him over the head with a colander, and put
weed killer in his elevenses.

Another thing I do is to find out All About It from a spiteful
friend who is giving me lunch in Claridge's. (It's always
Claridge's to allow me to bite back the lump in my throat on a

champagne cocktail.) Anyhow I find out from this friend that he's been having it off with a blonde in a red maxi, and it's the big thing, and everyone knows about it except me.

Well, after that, I don't delay. I go home and pick up the dogs and the drawing room clock, and I withdraw all my half of the money from the bank, and then I go and tell Worcester that if anything happens she is to tell him that I loved him. After that I go and live in Ireland in obscurity, until one day on a cold and stormy night as I'm playing the piano the door bursts open and it's Clever Drawers who has spent the last five years searching for me.

Actually that's my favourite. There are only two things which are difficult to gloss over. One is the fact that Worcester would send me straight home again. And the other is I can't play the piano. Well at least I can, but only the 'Trotting Pony', which isn't really what you'd call bursting into a room music. Still I could always learn something else. No really. Nothing's too much trouble when there's a blonde in a red maxi about.

5

Clever Drawers thought it would be lovely to have a baby, and so did I. We both imagined this gorgeous gurgling creature chuckling in a high chair just like on the advertisements. Well that was all right – until I started being sick. Then we suddenly realized that we didn't know anything about anything.

The trouble was that no one had told us people didn't feel well when they were having babies. As far as we knew they came home with mystical looks on their faces and started knitting things, and then when Cary Grant or Spencer Tracy came through the door they stopped them in their tracks with 'darling, I've got something to tell you . . . '

I must say I used to dream about that all the time when I was at school. Right through double Latin on Monday afternoons I would imagine myself floating down the stairs and saying when I reached the bottom step 'darling I've got something to tell you . . . ' Or 'I've been to see Dr Jones' dot, dot, dot, and then having to get no further, because hardly had I said that when Cary Grant/Spencer Tracy was kneeling at my feet Humbled.

After that I would spend nine months looking serene and knitting in a rocking chair – not being sick and getting spots – which is actually what happened.

Clever Drawers was just as confused as me about the whole thing, and he's been to University so he's no slouch, if you know what I mean. Although at the time I was dreaming through double Latin he was cutting out pictures of Cyd Charisse's legs – nevertheless even he thought people said 'darling I've got something to tell you . . . ' Then suddenly realized that it must be a pretty funny 'would you like a cocktail my dear?' sort of set-up if she had to tell him. I mean so where had he been all her life?

Of course we were pretty banjaxed by the whole business –

particularly the spots. The thing is all my life, through fat and thin, short and squat – I've been able to say 'well at least I've never had spots', and now here I was getting fatter by the minute and covered in spots. No serene and shining skin glowing with the knowledge that I was fulfilling my Greatest Role. No evidence that I had become part of the miracle of life, only hours spent with my head bent over the basin, and skin like a currant bun.

I never realized that having a baby meant you had to go to hospital. I thought you just knitted and knitted, and on the day the doctor told you – it arrived – not exactly by stork – but nearly.

I'd never been inside a hospital before. My knees knocked like there was no tomorrow, and just telling the nurse my name and address seemed like joining the Foreign Legion. Just for a few minutes I thought I didn't want to have a baby after all. I mean I'd nothing against the baby – it was just that it suddenly didn't seem as easy as buying a dog, and I thought perhaps I might not have what it took. Then I realized that that was the worst thing about having a baby – you can't change your mind. I mean it's not like a holiday to the Costa Brava – you can't just cancel it and pay a booking charge. I said this to the nurse, but she kept on saying 'where's your specimen?' as if anyone who is anyone always walks about with specimens in their handbags. Nurses can be pretty funny like that.

Still after a bit I stopped being sick, and got quite cheery. I was bursting out of everything so Clever Drawers took me off on a tour of the Maternity Shops. He was extraordinary really. He hadn't lost one of his bad habits. I mean I should have thought – in view of my condition -- that he would have calmed down a bit about fashion, but not at all. He insisted on coming into the changing room with me – although it was a dreadful squash – and then kept on charging in and out talking about 'room for growth', as if he'd given birth to nineteen children, and brought them all up by hand himself.

It wasn't enough for him to stick to the dress section either. In the space of about one minute he became an expert on maternity girdles, elastic stockings, and nursing bras. He kept leaping in and out of the cubicle with his hands full, and the assistant kept on saying how nice it was to find a young man who took such an Interest. To which old Clever Drawers would reply 'I think men Should' as he narrowed his eyes and muttered 'room for growth' for the hundredth time.

In the end he kitted me out with enough dresses, and bras and girdles to see me through three pregnancies. It was no use telling him the elastic stockings were for varicose veins – he just muttered 'well you never know' and looked hopefully at my legs.

All the way home on the underground he kept shouting 'look' as someone got in with a baby. But that was nothing compared to the way his eyes would fill with tears when the Heinz baby started gurgling on television, and he would pace up and down the room shouting 'I can't believe it', in between scrutinizing Dr Spock as if it was the Good Food Guide.

I kept on bursting into tears too. I would sit in the kitchen for hours on end with tea towels on my head sobbing about how awful everything was, and then I'd rush out and buy a doughnut and eat it before Clever Drawers came home, because he was very strict about diet – and rubbing yourself with oil – and going to Class.

Class meant having to be taught All about Babies and How To Have Them. I'm not very good at that sort of group activity. There's something about me that doesn't encourage other women. Worcester says some girls are women, and some girls are birds, and if you're more bird than woman, you tend not to get on with women.

The first thing you notice when you go into a room full of pregnant women is everyone looking around at everyone else thinking 'How Did *She* Get Pregnant' and 'How Awful To Be *That* Shape'.

Actually you don't quite understand what nature can do to you until you're in a whole room full of pregnancies. I mean some people carry babies round about their knees, some under their chins, and others look as if someone's pinned some washing on their fronts, and they don't have anything to do with what's attached to them.

So anyway, for the first class everyone arrived with tights and jumpers – except me – because I'd left my jumper on the bus. I don't know why, I have this knack of starting off on the wrong foot. My very first school I was the only one with a velvet beret, and everyone called me 'poshy'. Another thing – there's something about my face that makes people want to make a demonstration out of me. Perhaps it's because I'm always in the wrong clothes, or perhaps I've got that know-it-all look that asks for people to squash you. Anyway standing in the middle of the room surrounded by all those other women, I kept on remembering large girls with red legs saying to me on the first day of term 'you're going to be *squashed*'.

I went redder and redder as the teacher said for the fifteenth time 'don't you know where your knees are? I said bend your knees – not flap your hands' and all the others laughed into their knitting wool. And then the teacher looked round the room and said in that dead tired voice – 'is there anyone here who knows where their knees are?' And I had to go and sit down against the wall knowing that everyone else knew that I didn't even know where my *knees* were for heaven's sake. I mean you can feel people staring at a person who doesn't know where their knees are. You can hear them thinking 'if she doesn't know where her knees are – how on earth's she going to Cope?' Question mark, question mark.

The next thing we had to do was lie about the floor and relax. The principal of this being that when the time comes to give birth you will be all happy and lovely and not yelling your head off and biting your teeth on a strap like you've always understood from the movies. Anyway what happens is that you stiffen your arm or your leg and that is a pretend pain, and then you make the rest of you relaxed and you puff and blow to a smaller or a greater degree according to how much pain you're meant to be having, if you know what I mean.

It's not as easy as it sounds, particularly if you're the sort of person who doesn't know where their knees are, and tends to stiffen their breath and relax their arm. The teacher kept on coming round to me and saying 'I can see I'll have to do a lot of work on you', which makes you feel far from better.

Things didn't improve when she got out the Birth Atlas, and

I kept looking away, and she kept saying 'I suppose you know all about the placenta? I mean I suppose we have nothing to teach you?' Which are the sort of questions that make 'yes' and 'no' the wrong answer – so you say 'blurp' instead, and everyone else stares at the wrinkles on their tights, or looks keenly at the picture of the placenta to prove how different they are from you.

If you don't like thinking about parts of the body, you are not ideal material for having babies. You can't explain that to teachers and people, because they think everything to do with the body is wonderful. And if you said 'I think the placenta looks revolting' they'd immediately go into the 'do you realize how lucky you are to have one?' line of thinking – 'I mean I suppose you know what it's like *not* to have one?' which makes you look warped, and the sort of person who doesn't deserve to *experience* childbirth.

Anyway all the way home on the bus I kept practising stiffening my arm and straightening my leg and doing my breathing, which succeeded in emptying the top deck quicker than anything you've ever seen, so much so that whenever Clever Drawers wanted a seat on the underground afterwards he'd just say 'quick do your breathing' and in a second we'd have a carriage to ourselves. I don't know why, but there's something about a pregnant woman stiffening her arm which puts people off.

Actually the best way to keep cheerful when you're having a baby is never to look at yourself sideways. This is the crux of the matter. If you can get through nine months without ever looking sideways you will keep smiling. It's much easier to say than to do. I mean you might not feel tempted to spend hours looking sideways at yourself when you're at home, but when you're trotting along the road and there's a breeze blowing and you catch sight of yourself in a shop window, you can suddenly feel very distressed. Just for a moment it doesn't seem possible for anyone to be that shape and Human.

And it's no good people telling you that in Italy you would be treated like a sacred cow, that doesn't help one bit, because in England you are treated like the noun – without the adjective. I mean to be openly pregnant in public is an offence. It's as if no one else has been born that way, or that you are some sort of freak. People in shops make remarks, and stare at your hand to see if you've got a nice gold band on. Old ladies are the worst. They can't wait to slam swing doors on your stomach and bash you with their handbags, because to them you are a blatant example of someone who's had sex and Doesn't Mind Who Knows It. Exclamation mark, exclamation mark.

Sometimes I used to wish I'd been one of those people who won't have babies because of the Atom Bomb. Not when I was out with Clever Drawers and he was rushing up and down baby departments trying out the gears on prams as if they were Jensens, but when I was sitting in a heap at parties watching sticky thin girls, or when I got one of those 'I'll never be Free again' days on. Actually they were usually brought about by going to see someone who actually had a baby.

There is nothing worse when you are about to give birth than going to see someone who just has. By the time they've finished removing the nappies from your cup of tea you feel like running out and throwing yourself under a tree.

They always look at you with their heads on one side as if they've been midwives for twenty years, instead of just having given birth to one measly infant, and say things like 'have they X-rayed for twins?' Or 'have you *always* been that shape?' And then with relish they tell you all about how the worst bit is the Injection, or 'I do hope you don't have to be induced' and they talk about 'the drip' as if it was the rack. Then to prove how awful being a mother is they let bits of Marmite fingers drop out of their mouths while they're talking, and undo their bandages to show you their varicose veins.

Clever Drawers used to sit up all night with me as we promised ourselves that we would never become like Them. We wouldn't ever let nappies spill out of the bucket, or leave potties to perfume the hall, or kiss babies' bottoms, or breast feed during dinner parties. The thought of being reduced to talking about Dr Spock and gripe water haunted us, and we spent hours hovering outside Woolworths peering into prams in an effort to harden ourselves to just how ugly babies could be.

Sometimes Clever Drawers would pretend that he wasn't really afraid of Becoming Like Them. 'I know hundreds of people who've had babies who are still all right,' he'd say grandly, but that's as far as he ever got because he could never ever remember who they were, and would end up saying hopelessly 'well, we don't *have* to get like other people.'

Mind you there wasn't much risk of that in some ways. Particularly not with my memory. I know it doesn't sound like it, but not having a memory can be a grave handicap, particularly when you're Expecting. If it's not this it's that, and no sooner have you finished rubbing oil over you than you have to go to class, and as soon as you've finished class you have to go to hospital. One day I forgot my specimen jar so I took it along in an old Miss Dior bottle, and the nurse nearly fainted because when she stuck the piece of paper in it turned green.

Then we both went and forgot what day it was meant to be born. I don't know what it was, I think we were both hoping the other person would remember, but when we woke up one morning – it was suddenly due tomorrow.

And then tomorrow was today, and Clever Drawers was marching up and down and saying 'well?' every five minutes, and if I let out a breath in order to get an intake of oxygen he'd shout 'relax, relax, remember what you've been taught', and then when nothing happened he kept making helpful suggestions like 'how about a nice cold beer and a hot bath?' Or 'I told you if you packed your suitcase it wouldn't arrive' – as if babies were out to spite you from the start.

Even when I went to the hospital they did nothing to cheer me up. 'What – you still here?' they kept saying as if I was holding up the National Health on purpose. I've never felt such a failure in my life, not even when I failed Grade One Music three times.

When I got home I put a tea towel on my head, until Clever Drawers came up with one of his Ideas. Since, he said, I had been so Foolish as to pack my suitcase and obviously Baby had taken note of this, we would now outwit Baby by giving a nonstop party so that Baby would be fooled into thinking we didn't expect it – because Babies were probably like casting directors – they only wanted you if you were too busy to care.

That sounded a good wheeze, and since Clever Drawers had

a craze on playing racing cars – we gave a racing car party. Racing car parties mean that everyone lies on the floor and swears at each other. This was a little more difficult for me than it was for everyone else, so I was shoved into a chair and told to chart the laps. Being a lap counter means that instead of just your own team, everyone in the room swears at you.

Not too many races had gone when I realized this was It. This was what it was all about. This was what all the classes had been for, about, to, or from, so I started to puff and blow just like I'd been taught – the only trouble was that no one had taught me how to puff and blow, and count the laps, so I kept on miscounting between puffs, and everyone kept shouting and Clever Drawers kept saying 'do stop panting and COUNT'.

Once or twice I said to anyone I thought was listening 'I'm in labour you know' – but no one noticed that my bump had slipped down to where my knees used to be. Only when we retired to the pub in the evening and all the little Irish girls behind the bar started to cross themselves and murmur 'there's going to be a miracle in Finch's' did anyone believe me, and then they all kept shouting 'you shouldn't be here' and snatching my drink away, which was a lot of use.

In the end they all came with us to the hospital, principally because it was closing time. Then they all went home again leaving me to watch television with the nurse who kept saying '*which* one was the father did you say?'

After a few hours I was being pushed down the corridor to the labour ward, and Clever Drawers and company were following on in their white coats and masks, and Sister was saying 'I really must insist that only *you* come in, Mr Danby – this isn't a pyjama party you know', and the ward doors closed to shouts of 'five to two it's a girl'.

Clever Drawers said to the anaesthetist 'I'll give you three to one because I like your eyes'.

Then the next bit was a little boring. Just me puffing and blowing, and Clever Drawers muttering to the nurse 'do you come here often?' in his best Groucho Marx, and Sister saying 'if you want to *see* anything you'd better put your glasses *inside* your mask', and then suddenly Clever Drawers had hold of my hand and said 'come on pet I've got a lot of money on you', and Sister said 'there we are' and there was a cry like a shout in Spring, and everyone burst into tears because there's something about a pink and crumply face which gets you in the end. No Honestly.

6

Every time Clever Drawers was out of work I used to say to him 'why don't you go and shout at someone – like that actor I told you about?' I think the reason he didn't kill me every time I said it was because it had become part of our routine. In between listening for the telephone to ring – I said either 'why don't you go and shout at someone?' or 'perhaps you ought to go to a football match?'

Going to a football match like everyone else was our idea of the ultimate in degradation. The purpose in going was that lots of so-called directors were meant to be going to football matches in those days, and lots of so-called actors, were, it was rumoured, getting work from going to football matches. We used to cut out pictures of directors and stick them up in the kitchen with 'Would You Go To A Football Match With This Man?' underneath.

I used to think being out of work could be quite romantic, but after the ninety-ninth leap to the phone you start to wonder a little bit. For one thing it's boring, and for another thing everywhere you go you keep hearing bells in your head. I mean the slightest sound could be Hollywood at last, although it's more likely to be the bell on the dog's collar.

Besides leaping about every time you think you hear a bell you also have this pathetic idea that no one else knows that you're out of work. One of our drawbacks was that we weren't even out of work in a with-it kind of way. Our style of Pretending It's Not Happening went out with Noël and Gertie. We used to rush about buying the first round, and saying things like 'well there is something we're waiting to hear about' – when all that we were waiting to hear about was our bank balance.

When we weren't in the pub comparing how long who'd been

out of work – we were lying staring at the ceiling with our hands behind our heads saying 'this isn't going to get us anywhere' or 'well we can always sell the house', and after one of us had said that the other one would say crossly 'that won't help' – which in a way was true, because even money doesn't help you to decide whether or not to Give It All Up. And anyway Clever Drawers said you couldn't give something up if it had given you up – so even wondering that was pretty pointless.

Sometimes the phone would actually ring, and we would fall over each other ironing shirts and straightening ties, and trying to make Clever Drawers look the part which is usually pathetic, because nine times out of ten the secretary's got her shorthand wrong, and he would turn up in mohair and silk when what they wanted was six o'clock shadow and holes in his jumper.

Every time he went off on one of those pathetic trips I used to think he'd be a star by the following morning. I mean that's exactly how stupid I was. He hadn't even caught the bus to go and stand with ten other people in a draughty corridor, and I'd have re-decorated the house. And by the time he got back I'd written 'My Life With A Star' and sold it all over the world.

At one point it actually stopped being funny. At one point every time Clever Drawers went to the cupboard to put on his audition gear, he somehow always came away looking run-over, and I used to say irritating things like 'I don't think that shirt's quite right you know', and he would shout 'what's wrong with it?'

'Well it makes you look *green*.'

'What do you mean it makes me look green? What kind of green?'

'Well no particular kind of green – just green.'

'You can't look just "green". Either you look dark green, or light green, or peppermint green – green is never *just* "green".'

'Well all right – grass green then.'

At this point he would peer in the mirror and then come back.

'Can you honestly sit there and tell me that I look the colour of grass? I mean do you really mean to say IN ALL SERIOUSNESS that I look the colour of that grass growing out there?'

'Well not exactly – but nearly.'

11

'What do you mean not exactly but *nearly*. I mean either I look grass green – or I don't. I mean did you or did you not say I looked "grass" green?'

'Well yes – in a way but only because you *made* me.'

But by that time he would be half-way down the road leaving me to mutter about people with University educations who can't be happy with green being green like everyone else – they have to make a *fuss* about it. And then when he got back there was usually nothing else to do but add yet another name to our 'When I'm Head of the World' list.

If you're going to be out of work you need a 'When I'm Head of the World' list. You not only need one, it's completely necessary for your sanity. If you don't have a 'When I'm Head of the World' list you will drown in your own fury, which probably could be a fate worse than death.

People tend to get very tiny minded when they're out of work because it seems that everyone else in the world is doing something interesting except you, and you spend the whole time trying not to watch television because if you do you go out of your mind every time someone you can't stand appears. In fact the best thing you can do when you're out of work is to stay in bed, because then you won't be tempted to spend money or lose your temper. It's very difficult to lose your temper when you're lying down.

Actually I used to think Clever Drawers was exaggerating about how slaggy everything was, and then I realized that not only was he not exaggerating, he was just putting it mildly, as it were. It didn't matter how well you read at auditions there was usually only the stage manager listening – if you were lucky – everyone else was blowing their noses or scratching their spots. Not only that but they usually had someone signed up already, so the whole thing was a waste of time, and they couldn't care less if you'd travelled all the way from Yorkshire – they'd just carry on blowing their noses.

People don't mind what they do to you at auditions, and the only time they're really interested is if you're rude. If you're rude to someone at auditions everyone will fall about laughing and employ you straight away, because that means you must be talented. The theory is that only talented people are rude, so if you want to get a part nine times out of ten the best way to do it is to make a vee sign, and employment will be yours.

There used to be a great vogue for tables and chairs at auditions. The number of times Clever Drawers had to improvise being a table or a chair, or a tramp at a party. It was no good me saying 'what's that got to do with *Othello*?' all the time, because no one could tell you. All they said was it was very relaxing. Clever Drawers didn't find it relaxing, but then he would insist on being a gate-legged table – and that is very tiring.

One day I said 'I wish I could see your gate-legged table in action', so he said 'why don't you?', because things had gone from being funny to serious – back to funny again.

All the way there on the bus I said 'supposing they ask me who I am?' But he only said 'they won't – they never do', because he has a great deal of enviable cool like that, and when I'm busy making my plea from the dock he's wondering what will win the three-thirty.

Just before we got to the stage door I said to him 'give me your brief case – I'll say I'm Miss Wantage – your personal assistant. I'll say you never audition without me.'

'Oh, all right,' he said, very bored.

I looked at the ground all the time he was saying his name to the man at the stage door, and then made very draggy personal assistant type noises as I followed him down to the basement. I unclipped the brief case and handed him his script, then I took out a notebook and pretended to study it. Clever Drawers muttered 'there's no need to overdo it you know', because I'd started to rub my nose with a Kleenex and make my ears stick through my hair.

When I dared to I had a look round the room, and I must say it was worth it. There was everything there from puss in boots to Tarka the otter – and all for the part of a car salesman. Clever Drawers cleared his throat once or twice, and I said 'I wonder if they'll ask you for your gate-legged table?' and he said 'shut up', because once I start talking in public he's afraid I'll never stop – which I very often don't.

After that the stage manageress came into the room and called

Clever Drawers' name. We followed her up to the wings, and I stood beside her while he did his 'Hallo love' exchange to the faceless wonders in the stalls. The stage manageress had a very bad cold and a cardigan like an ambulance blanket. She said something to me which I couldn't make out, and then she went on stage, and I realized that she was going to read the other parts against Clever Drawers. With her cold I didn't think it was going to be funny. After a couple of minutes someone said 'thank you very much'. Dot, dot, dot.

And that was it.

On the bus home I said 'I'm sorry they didn't ask for your gate-legged table.' And Clever Drawers said 'Do you see what I mean?' And I said 'Yes. I mean you couldn't even have been rude could you? I mean it was too slaggy even to make a vee sign or something. Not even Marlon Brando could have got that job with that going on, could he?' Clever Drawers said 'Well – perhaps Brando, but not much else – ' because he likes Marlon's acting a lot.

I looked out of the window after that, and I added a few more names to my 'When I'm Head of the World' list.

Of course the good thing was that I had actually seen for myself. I mean it was all very well me sitting at home like Marjorie Morningstar saying 'Why don't you *shout* at someone', or 'You could be rude if you tried', but until you've seen how unconducive things can be, you're talking through your well-known hat. Anyway I don't see how anybody in their right minds can be expected to give of their best and be a convincing car salesman, if there's someone sneezing down their ear hole.

That evening we came to a few conclusions. We realized that Clever Drawers was just Not the Type to go to football matches, or to prop up the bar in the Salisbury, or to become a poof, all of which recourses have been known to Work. But on the other hand this did not stop him hustling just like anyone else, so we decided hustling was all right so long as it wasn't at football matches, in bars, or with homosexuals. Then we decided it was a good thing to Get Up. In fact we voted unanimously for Getting Up. Not Getting Up, we decided, did not improve things. Also doing exercises, and not eating too much, because thin people look better on the credits.

All these decisions were very good news. We stopped lying looking at the ceiling with our hands behind our heads saying 'this isn't going to get us anywhere' and got up very early, had breakfast, did our exercises, and sat looking at each other saying 'this isn't going to get us anywhere'.

Still we were absolutely determined to hustle. I mean as far as we were concerned, football-matches-bars-and-poofs apart, if everyone else could hustle, so could we. We spent a long time polishing up our brass necks in preparation for the Big Hustle. The very next time we were asked to what insurance men call a Show Biz Party, we would plan our campaign – we would leave no crisp unturned, no olive unswivelled, no joke unpolished in our scramble for power.

By the time the invitation came through the post I had already called Sam Spiegel and told him to up his offer by another million. Sammy Glick had nothing on me. I could see myself – always one jump ahead – wisecracking with the tough guys – the Broad with the Brain.

'Course it's not quite the same when you get there and all you can see is a row of backs, and a good deal of front, which is what you're hoping to have.

Actually that's one good thing about Clever Drawers, he is very good crack at a Do. I mean he can't help it if women go after him all the time, but when they're not, the old fruit can make a party out of thin air. Mind you the conversation is usually a trifle tinged, or what Worcester would call 'un peu bleu' but that's a good thing, because if anyone sees a man and a woman laughing together they always assume you can't be married and leave you alone.

Everyone left us alone that evening, so there was nothing to do but start the hustling unaided. Clever Drawers chose me a fat man with a cigar who, he said, had to be a producer, and I chose him a red-headed bird, because she had such a large diamond she had to be 'Somebody's' Girl friend, and anyway I knew Clever Drawers couldn't afford her.

Luckily for me the must-be-producer was sitting by himself

on a sofa, and although he was fat and so was I, there was enough room for us both if I held my breath.

I said 'hallo' in a squashed kind of way, and he nodded and pushed some peanuts at me. Eating peanuts and getting only nods in reply to my attempts at conversation I didn't feel much like Sammy Glick. In fact I felt more like moving, but then I remembered the purpose of my journey from the other side of the room, and I persevered. As long as I kept on talking, I realized, he would have to keep on sitting, and as long as he kept on sitting the better chance I had of insinuating myself into his orb and thereby get to mentioning Clever Drawers and his talent, and everything.

Every time I suspected he was about to move I renewed the pace of my conversation, and in the midst of my Thoughts On Today's Cinema and Television Today, I couldn't help thinking that even Sammy Glick couldn't have talked *faster*. I mean he might have talked better, more to the purpose, but not *faster*.

Eventually when I stopped he said 'Well now you've told me all about show business, would you like to hear a little about civil engineering?'

An hour later I met Clever Drawers behind the appointed aspidistra. I said 'Listen, if you ever want to build a few bridges I've got just the man for you.'

He hadn't got on much better. Mademoiselle of the diamond had proved to be an ardent devotee of stock car racing, and newly engaged to a stuntman who was due to join her any minute, so Clever Drawers after a little desultory exchange of prangs had beaten a hasty retreat – stuntmen not being notorious for their flower power.

'Do you know I don't think we're very good at hustling,' said Clever Drawers gloomily.

I could see his point of view, so we went in search of some food. And then we found a good picnic spot in the shape of a linen cupboard.

'We just mustn't be got down,' I said between mouthfuls.

Clever Drawers agreed.

'Nor must we type cast too heavily. I mean producers could

be tall, thin, and teetotal. They don't have to be small, fat, and smoke cigars.'

'They usually are though.'

'So are civil engineers.'

'And stock car enthusiasts.'

'She didn't smoke a cigar did she?'

'No, but you know what I mean.'

'Yes. Well I suppose we'd better pack up and dive into the fray again. Bon chance, and all that.'

'Up the Argylls.'

Clever Drawers turned away stepping into another small fat man with a cigar. He made an impeccable apology.

'Goddam Limey, in your goddam military jacket. What do you want to wear a jacket like that for?'

Clever Drawers looked down at him, and started to walk on.

'Goddam Limeys – never talk to anyone.'

He turned. 'Sir,' he said, 'if you wish to insult the English that is your affair, but – if on the other hand you wish to insult me, perhaps you should know that I am YORKSHIRE.'

I thought that was quite neat. It didn't stop old cigar-face.

'Goddam Yorkshire then – what the hell's a goddam Yorkshire man doing over here?'

'Living off the fat of the land – same as you – you ridiculous Polish exile.'

That caught cigar-face a sting. He seized Clever Drawers' lapels, and I was glad he was so small – in view of Clever Drawers being a pacifist. 'Hungarian,' he screamed.

'You ridiculous Hungarian exile.'

'Let me tell you – you Yorkshire bum – I've been a citizen of the United States of America for thirty years.'

'I don't care if you've been engaged to Lon Chaney for thirty years – I don't like being called a Limey by a Polish –'

'HUNGARIAN!'

'Sorry – by a Hungarian exile.'

'Oh don't you –'

'No, and please stop swinging from my jacket.'

'Very well Yorkshire bum – but just remember Hungarian is not Polish.'

167

'And just you remember Yorkshire bums are not goddam Limeys.'

'You're the first goddam human being I've met this evening, Yorkshire bum.'

They shook hands.

'Thank you.'

'It's a pleasure.'

He waddled off, and we went home, because Clever Drawers says you should always leave when the going's good, and anyway somehow things hadn't quite worked out as we had planned, which things have a habit of doing when you try planning them. The unexpected is the magic ingredient which makes all the buildings have windows again.

Still, as I said to Clever Drawers the next day – in between staring at each other and saying 'this isn't going to get us anywhere' – at least we *tried*. I mean at least we did try and hustle, even if all it got us was an earful of stock car racing, and an intimate knowledge of how to build a suspension bridge.

The telephone rang, and we pretended we weren't really interested. I picked up the receiver very very slowly, because I like to pretend to the people the other end that I am so BUSY that I can only answer after I've put down the Other receiver. Just as I like to pretend I'm a Lady Executive with long nails by dialling with my biro. Anyway I said 'Yes?' instead of 'Hallo?' – which I always find cool.

'Yorkshire bum?'

'No.'

'Is that Yorkshire bum's house?'

'Yes.'

'Tell him to come to Park Lane and see me, Beatrice has the details. Three o'clock this afternoon.'

He put the phone down. Our mouths dropped open. Just as we were shutting them the phone rang again.

'Yes?'

'You come too.'

I paced about the room while Clever Drawers was phoning Beatrice. Who was Polish Exile and why did he want Yorkshire bum and me to go and see him? I couldn't wait for next week's instalment.

'It was only Otto Klepinoff.'

'Not *the* Otto Klepinoff? Not the Otto Klepinoff that neither of us have heard of?'

'The very same.'

'What does he want?'

'Our bodies.'

'That's all right then.'

We tiptoed down endless corridors and then arrived at Mr Klepinoff's door. No one answered the first ring, but when we rang again the door opened – very narrowly – and a small blonde eyed us.

'Who are you?' she asked in American.

'The Danbys,' said Clever Drawers bravely.

She shut the door again. A minute later she re-opened it.

'Have you an appointment, Mr Randy?'

'Danby. Yes. With Mr Klepinoff.'

'Oh. Well, you'd better come in.'

She opened the door wider, but not too wide. She obviously didn't like fat people.

After we had squeezed through she stood looking at us as if she wasn't quite sure how we had got in, and then she said: 'Let me take your coats,' which made me glad that we'd put on our Good ones, even though what was underneath wasn't exactly joosh. She put down the coats very slowly, and then said: 'Would you like a drink?' which did a lot to bring a look of keenness to our faces. We both said 'Brandy please,' because that's another rule when you're out of work. Always ask for the drink you can't afford.

After that we didn't know whether to stay looking at the coats, which we had after all seen before, or carry on into the main room as if she'd asked us to, which she hadn't. Eventually we decided to carry on, under the assumption that no one offers you a brandy if they want you to leave immediately.

She came back a few minutes later very quietly, very slowly, with two very large brandies. Then she went into another room, and we heard her say 'Otto – some people called the Randys are here.'

'Hallo Yorkshire bum.'

'Hallo Mr Klepinoff.'

'Good to see you Yorkshire bum.'

'Good to see you Mr Klepinoff.'

'Will you have a drink?'

'No, thank you. That is, we've got one.'

'Good. Listen I shan't be a minute. Will you excuse me?'

Quarter of an hour later Mr Klepinoff came back.

'Yorkshire bum.'

'Mr Klepinoff.'

'It's good to see you.'

'Thank you very much.'

'You were the only human being I met last night. The only goddam human being.'

'Thank you Mr Klepinoff.'

'Sit down. Have another drink.'

I watched Mr Klepinoff. He was amazing, not just because I'd had two brandies, he was amazing in his own right. He could take a puff of his cigar, chew his gum, spit and then drink – all at the same time. And he never once lost the sequence. Just watching him made me envious. I mean this could be the secret of his power. I mean this could be the reason Klepinoffs became Klepinoffs.

His voice had taken on a deep and serious level, because he was talking about how much money he had invested in his recent picture. I was trying to work it back from dollars into pounds, but I kept on putting the point in the wrong place. Clever Drawers was trying to work the conversation round to asking why we were here. Our imaginations had run from the star having a heart attack, to the writer being sacked, back to the star having a heart attack.

Eventually Mr Klepinoff said – puff, chew, spit, drink, 'Yorkshire bum, I expect you're wondering why we've asked you here? And I expect er – is wondering why as well, aren't you – ? Well I'm going to tell you. There's a scene in my picture, in the script, that I want you two to be in. It needs you, it needs the real thing, if you know what I mean. It needs authentiquity. When I saw you last night, apart from the fact that you were the only goddam human being that I met the whole evening, apart from that, I realized that you were what this scene NEEDS. This scene cries out for someone like you, in that goddam stupid jacket standing around with a bird, are you with me Yorkshire bum?'

'Perhaps you could tell us a little more Mr Klepinoff?'

'Yes, well this situation is such that there is a big swanky party going on downstairs in this big swanky house, and the bird and the guy are up in the bedroom – if you get my meaning? And downstairs you and people like you are milling around, if you understand me – milling around – with edge.' He paused. 'This is going to be a Q for quality picture, Yorkshire bum, Q for quality and I want you to help me in this.'

I believe the expression is 'a mixture of emotions', anyway quite a lot of these floated across our faces. Sorrow that the star was still healthy, and the writer still in favour, and at the same times gratitude that Mr Klepinoff thought we had Q for quality.

When we got outside Clever Drawers said, 'This could be your big break, baby. You've always wanted to be a movie star – so now's your chance.'

'Shut up.'

When the day of my big break arrived the make-up girl eyed me with disfavour. Make-up girls usually do. They can smell out the messy dresser in me. They know I don't really care. They can see I'm one of those people who try and get by, try and make do.

Her eyes narrowed in the mirror as if she suspected me of spitting in the mascara. 'I'll have to take some of those eyebrows off,' she said, 'and I'll try and tone your nose down.'

I saw the eyes of the three girls sitting behind me swivel towards my nose, not my best feature at the best of times, but on this early Sunday morning it had assumed the proportions of Mont Blanc. I wished now that I had been more dedicated about my face. Now that it was too late I wished I'd toned where it obviously cried out for toning, varnished, smoothed, plucked, bleached myself fit for the wide screen. I mean you could see those three pairs of eyes thinking 'And she thinks she's going to be in a film with those eyebrows and THAT nose!'

'Do you want anything done about your hair?' The make-up girl switched on the electric rollers without waiting for a reply.

I shut my eyes, but I could feel the attention, the interest, from behind was on those eyebrows and that nose. I hoped that when I opened them again I would see my face as I'd like others to see it. That I'd see a browless noseless face fit for Technicolored Amplavision.

Clever Drawers put his paper cup of coffee down.

'What on earth have they done to you?'

'What do you mean what on earth have they done to me?' I said crossly, because he has this irritating habit of always putting the obvious into very loud sentences.

'You look like Coco the clown.'

'I've brought a hat with me, I'll just have to pull it down over my face.'

'You can't wear a HAT.'

'Why ever not?'

'Because it's in the evening, and it's after dinner, that's why ever not.'

'Well I'll just have to build up my part into "Lady with Hat" instead of "Lady".'

'At least you don't have any lines.'

Clever Drawers raised his eyes to heaven in that way people do when they know they are old hands and you're the new girl. 'Just remember not to UTTER when the voice says ACTION! – until you hear another voice saying "CUT" – see?'

I nodded. I had put my hat on which made me feel better. I pulled it down over my face. I hoped I felt trendy, and knew I didn't. Lots of people wear hats at dinner and parties and things, I told myself reassuringly. There obviously were certain circumstances when I would wear a hat at dinner, just because I couldn't think of any didn't mean they didn't exist.

The location was an empty house. A Regency house with a brass letter box and clean steps. It looked like an old actress who'd seen brighter days. Technicians stood about smoking in the hall beside a large tea urn. I sat down with the other girls while Clever Drawers went upstairs. He had lines, and close-ups and they were just about to do his scene.

I sat on my own. The other girls were giggling in the corner. They were old hands schooled in the art of how to do nothing well. One of the technicians nodded towards them. 'Don't you smoke love?'

'No, I don't actually.'

'You must be the only bloody person on this unit who bloody don't. The other bloody day when we couldn't bloody film I said to my mate, this is the first film in bloody forty years that they don't bloody offer you bloody Scotch – but a bloody smoke of bleeding ruddy grass. Stupebloodyfying. That's what it is.'

'Absolutely,' I agreed, and when Clever Drawers came down during a break I whispered, 'those girls are smoking pot, you know,' because I like getting things in first.

'That's nothing to what's going on upstairs.'

He'd hardly said that when he was called again.

How can someone say that to you? I mean how can someone say that's nothing to what's going on upstairs, and then go away again. It was incredible. What was going on upstairs and why? With whom? And how?

'They're not smoking up there too are they?' I hissed when he came down again.

Clever Drawers stared straight ahead of him. 'Smoking – if that was all they were doing.'

'What do you mean "if that was all they were doing?" '

'Nothing.'

When people say nothing it usually means something. My mind turned to orgies. I don't know why but I can never imagine orgies in modern dress. No matter how hard I try my orgies are always full of centurions in breast plates. I gazed at the ceiling. At this very moment I imagined the room above us seething with activity, and that sort of manic laughter that is so hard to achieve.

It was time for my scene, or rather it was time for the scene I was in. Someone came up to me and said 'Are you going to wear that?' meaning my hat. The director called to me, 'Hey you – Titfer, I want you to walk towards me – yes, you – walk towards me and then go off to camera right – understand? Good.

'Right quiet everyone – start walking – Action!'

It isn't until you start doing something like walking towards a camera that you realize that it's much more complicated than you first realized. I mean it isn't until you start walking that you grow to appreciate the number of movements that go to make up a walk. Up until that minute you always thought walking was walking, you didn't realize it was a question of unsticking your legs in four different places, sliding your feet – with their shoes on – forward, and then replacing each foot where the other foot last was.

'All right. "Cut!" Titfer, would you mind going back to your mark and dropping the imitation of the blood-hound? You're at a party, not tracking escaped prisoners.'

On the eighth take I started to walk a bit better. I imagined myself at this fabulous party. In fact I was enjoying myself so much that when I saw Clever Drawers standing behind the camera – I waved. Just the sort of thing people do at parties I thought – rather inspired, and relaxed, a genuine piece of improvision for which I would reluctantly accept an Oscar.

'Cut!'

'What on earth did you do that for?' Clever Drawers grumbled. 'I don't know what you thought you were doing.'

'Improvising.'

'Improvising does not mean waving.'

I went and sat by the tea urn in the hall. My first big break, and they'd given the part to someone else. My first chance to really make an impression, to swing into shot in a cameo that could have made me, and here I was sitting by the tea urn listening to someone else doing it. Not only had I failed with that nose and those eyebrows, but I had waved. Bad enough to be lousing up a scene with that nose and those eyebrows, but to be waving as well. Dot, dot, dot, exclamation mark.

I stared at my feet to take my mind off my nose, because once you start thinking about your nose the situation can get out of hand. I said to myself a few times 'I must not improvise, I must not improvise,' and then someone stuck their head round the door and said 'Come on, it's the crowd scene.'

This was the scene Mr Klepinoff had had us in mind for. This was the whole reason we were here. Determined never to be caught improvising again I did what Clever Drawers did. When he did pretend chat, I did pretend chat, when he raised his glass to his lips I did the same, and I milled around. By take fourteen I had milling around sewn up, and I was back thanking my agent on Oscar night. Filming was easy. As a matter of fact with very little pressure I thought I could be persuaded to take it up as a second career.

I saw the director saying something to Clever Drawers who came back to me. 'Freddie says – '

I knew what he was about to say. He was about to tell me that having seen the sheer quality of my milling around, they would like me to do something with more depth, something that would Stretch me.

'Freddie says would you mind not bobbing about so much?'

I couldn't believe it. I looked at Clever Drawers. Was he inferring that my milling around was merely Bobbing About? Did they really think that my mill was merely a bob? Couldn't they see the technique behind my milling? Couldn't they see the sheer technical know-how that goes into that kind of milling? It was incredible.

'Of course, it's that kind of attitude that has brought the industry to its knees,' I thought as I did a restrained version of my milling around for take fifteen. 'It's the wastage of talented millers around like me that has finally taken its toll – they have no one to blame but themselves if skilled millers like myself go into Other Fields.'

After take fifteen we all went and sat round the tea urn again. I'd always heard that filming meant a lot of hanging around. We hung around all right. By the time it was three o'clock I was finding it difficult to keep awake. I kept on saying to Clever Drawers 'Why can't we go?' and he kept on saying 'Because we haven't been *told* we can.' He's very good like that, he always knows the form. Still I couldn't see why we shouldn't go, because they were now on to filming the bedroom scenes. Perhaps they wanted a few millers around later on. I imagined the director saying 'Bring back the one with the hat.' Perhaps I would be discovered before six o'clock. I yawned again.

The Lighting Cameraman came down the stairs. He went to the urn and poured himself a cup of tea. Then he turned round. 'Well,' he said to the hall 'that's the first time I've lit THAT.'

Everyone stopped yawning and looked at him. He didn't have to say any more. Someone said to Clever Drawers, 'One for the private collection no doubt.'

I looked round. Just for a second everyone had forgotten their cool. We were all imagining having to lie there – the hot lights, the clapper board, the technicians. Perhaps the sound of someone sneezing, or the flick of the cables across the floor. Shut out, perform, contort – not for Art, not for The Word – Brought To You By Courtesy of Amplavision, but to moan across the screen as an after-dinner entertainment, to send up the temperatures and to increase the saliva of small fat men with large cigars. What a way to earn your bread.

No one could quite think of what to say. There was the sort of silence where everyone's brains are working overtime, but nothing comes out. Just as I thought I might have something the Star came down the stairs in his dressing gown. The girl from the scene followed shortly afterwards. She threw herself at his back, 'I do love you, I do love you, I really do,' she kept saying. But he just kept on pouring out his tea.

7

I suppose it was because the dog had just gone to the Big Kennel in the Sky that Clever Drawers decided we were going to have a holiday. We must stop thinking Gone For Long Walkies type thoughts, and make up our minds to live. The dog would have wanted it.

He became enthusiastic. He can get very enthusiastic, even when he doesn't mean to. You never know when it's going to hit him, but when it does it's like a force nine gale, and you'll overhear him promising Anything. One day I overheard him promising Sean and Susie that he was longing to share a villa in Spain. Him of all people, he whose idea of a holiday is to drink Guinness and watch the rain falling down.

He strode about the house extolling the properties of the sun. He said we needed Vitamin C after the long English winter. Not only did we need it, he doubted very much whether we would last through another without it. He became quite mystical as he talked about cheap wine, and freshly caught fish, and little night clubs under the stars.

Of course the good thing was that it was all going to be so incredibly cheap. Which was a good thing, because we didn't appear to have enough money for it. Not having enough money is a difficult thing to get round. You can get round not having enough talent, or not being beautiful enough, but not having enough money is very difficult to get round. You can't improvise a healthy bank statement, nor can you make it up to give the impression of being there. It either is or it isn't.

In view of the fact that paying for the tickets might be a little difficult, I thought we ought to sell something. The only trouble was that we didn't have anything to sell, until I remembered Granny's Old Prints. They were nothing to do with Granny

12

actually, but Clever Drawers is always naming things. Boiled Milk, Obsolescence, Banana Split, it doesn't matter what I put on – he's got a name for it. Anyway the plan was for me to take the prints to Sotheby's where they would rock back on their heels, and offer me hundreds of pounds for them.

'They could be Rowlandson's you know,' said Clever Drawers wisely. 'They have more than a hint of Rowlandson about them to me.'

By the time I had got off the Underground train they had more than a hint – in fact they were definitely by him. I imagined the scenes in the sale room when they came on the market. The breathless hush on the closed circuit television as the price soared into six figures, the cool voice of the auctioneer – the headlines 'Will the Prints Stay in England?'

Of course I didn't plan to keep all the money for ourselves. I would give some of it away – just keep enough to get us to Spain and back.

The man in front of me had definitely engaged the Expert's interest. The Expert was muttering things like 'almost certainly' and 'I should be surprised if' Dot, dot, dot. He got out a special bag and put the object of his scrutiny in. Then he made a special note, and he marked a number on the envelope. I tightened my hold on Granny's Old Prints. Any minute now they too were going to get a special bag, and a number – he might even summon the security guard to escort them to the Vaults. A few yah boos sprang to my mind as they usually do when the prospect of Sudden Riches looms large. Yah boo to the man in the fish shop. I could see myself graciously descending from my maroon Bentley Convertible and buying up all his haddock – to throw at him.

'I'm not quite sure what you thought these were?' The Expert looked from the prints to me and back to the prints again.

'Rowlandson's,' I whispered.

He sighed. I could see I was being put in the Mad Old Lady with Paper Bag bracket. He kept his gaze on Granny's Old Prints. 'The best I can say about these is – they're prints.'

'I don't suppose you have any suggestions – as to what I could do with them I mean?'

He nodded and I realized that it would be just as well not to wait for his reply. You can get that feeling sometimes. I mean on the odd occasion you can realize that to hover, even for another second, could mean an Exchange. And while Clever Drawers is good at Exchanges, I am not. I am liable to burst into tears and accuse experts of being Anti-Rowlandson. Anyway I wouldn't have sold him Granny's Old Prints even if they were worth a million pounds, not even if he had crawled across Sotheby's on his hands and knees. People like him didn't deserve Granny's Old Prints. He was probably wrong. The way they went on you'd think it was impossible for them to be wrong. Granny's Old Prints were very likely more Rowlandson than Rowlandson. He was so busy putting things in paper bags and marking down numbers he probably didn't have the *time* to recognize a Rowlandson when he saw one.

Clever Drawers said it was all very well, but not having sold anything didn't get us any nearer to Spain. I could see his point. We didn't seem to have anything else to sell. The prospect of winey sunny days was slipping through our fingers for want of an object to sell, until I said 'the house'.

'What do you mean "the house"?'

'That's what we sell – the house. It's too small anyway.'

'Of course it is.'

'We'll sell the house and have a holiday.'

We were going to be thin, brown and on the credits. As I packed I could see it all. When we came back no one would dare not employ us. No one would risk not employing us, unless they wanted to become the laughing stock of the World, the Universe and Space.

We met Sean and Susie at the airport. We all clutched jumbo packets of disposable nappies, and our suitcases were filled with tinned ham and baked beans. This was all part of the incredibly cheap plan. Although the owner of the villa had assured us of the wonderful eating places nearby, we thought it might be even more incredibly cheap if we ate at the villa, on the odd evenings that we weren't out wining and dancing.

It was night, which was a good thing because Clever Drawers had never been on an aeroplane before. Sean bought a large bottle of Bourbon, and before long he could have been on a flying carpet for all he cared. Susie and I sat at the front of the aeroplane with the children. The air hostess gave us professionally reassuring smiles as we passed her on our twelfth visit to the lavatory.

'No you can't pull the flush again.' I could see that lovely starched maid waiting for us at the villa. A gentle personable soul who had a way with children, scooping them up, leaving us to enjoy our drinks while she played endless enchanting games, or rocked them to sleep singing ancient Spanish airs which told of days long ago.

We arrived. Clever Drawers looked at the plane taking off again. 'I still don't understand how they stay up.'

We settled ourselves down on the airport steps to wait for the hire car to arrive. Eventually after an hour and a half Sean said savagely, 'I'll give them "Service with a Smile".' The children played in the gravel below, occasionally standing up to wave their plastic knickers at us.

'Here it comes.'

'Where the hell's the roof rack?'

'He doesn't speak French.'

'Où est le roof rack?'

'The ROOF RACK.'

'For el suitcases.'

'We no cannot fit in without it.'

'In London – yes? In London we pay for the ROOF RACK. Comprenez?'

'You no got one? Well get one – you steaming bowl of paella.'

'How about that one over there?'

'See car over there? That one of your cars?'

'He says "yes".'

'Tell him we're taking the roof rack off it.'

Everything was all right now. All we had to do was to get ourselves to the villa, stopping perhaps for a jolly breakfast on the way at one of the many inviting cafés we had heard about. The sun was hotter now, and although we were squashed and hot, our hearts rose with it. This was what it was all about. This was Living. Clever Drawers and Sean sang. The children slept. Susie and I smiled at each other. Already I could see my bowl of coffee and the cold white glistening butter on the hot bread.

'Mention Mr Smith's name, that's what he said to do.'

'Mr Smith he tell us to come to you.'

'Ah, Señor SMEETH.' There were large smiles now. 'Señor SMEETH, ah yes.'

'Señor Smith say you do mighty fine breakfast.'

'I wish Sean would stop talking El Sombrero,' Susie sighed. The children both had their knickers off again. Two large au pairs sat at another table watching us with unblinking brown eyes as they slowly chewed their way round some crusts of bread.

'Ah si, Señor Smith?' The café owner was still smiling.

'Señor Smith said you make breakfast for us.'

'Si, si, breakfast. Tomorrow?'

'Oh all right tomorrow. It is a bit late.'

'You know the way to Señor Smith's villa?'

Approximately was the answer to that. After several wrong turnings, we found it. It didn't look much like the pictures, but then none of Mr Smith's pictures had actually shown a view of the villa. They had shown views from, and the road leading up to, but not the actual villa. Still since we were there at last, it would have been over critical to demand that the villa looked anything more than white. Or that the sea should be right under the balcony as he had inferred. Just because it was a few hundred feet below and it would take a mountaineer to reach it without breaking a leg, didn't mean to say he had been bending the truth, just being a little colourful.

Anyway no one can help being entranced by a view of blue sea and sky, and the sound of ice against glasses. We opened the first of our tins of ham and ate lunch. Clever Drawers looked at me. It was certainly worth selling the house for this. The children playing happily, the sound of the sea, large drinks, tall glasses.

'We must try and get this awning up after lunch,' said Sean, but the afternoon idyll was shattered when he raised his arm.

Normally raising your arm need not incur anything more disastrous than a slight creak from your shoulder, or a pull on the tummy muscles, but in Sean's case it extended to his back teeth and broke a bridge. Not many people keep bridges in their mouths, but Sean had several lying around on account of his being in the middle of having his teeth capped.

'Ah well,' he said philosophically, looking at it, 'I'll just have to eat on the other side. At least we got the awning up.'

The next problem was whether to go down to the beach or to the local club which rumour had it would supply us with Anything We Wanted. We all thought the beach, but Sean favoured the club. There was a wonderful pool there, and we could swim and drink, drink and swim, and anyway the beach might be a bit crowded.

The club looked just as good as Mr Smith had promised us. A large pool, a small pool, an inside bar, an outside bar, fairy lights, a place to dance. Idyllic. Clever Drawers looked at me. This too was certainly worth selling the house for. The children playing, the sound of diving, large drinks, tall glasses.

Again the idyll was shattered. This time by a large man in a cotton hat, 'Would you mind stopping your child doing that?' He pointed an outraged finger.

'Doing WHAT?' Susie bristled.

'I will not have people splashing water over the side.'

'Empty the pool then,' said Sean affably. The man backed away from him screaming. Sean watched him. 'One second longer and I'd have shown him my back teeth.'

In fact his back teeth became the subject of some discussion the next morning. He had toothache. Not on the side where the bridge had broken, but on the side where he could display four or five gleaming white caps. Everyone's reaction was much the same. Toothache we all agreed was awful, but with a few aspirins and a few drinks he would probably be fine. After all the ache being on the side it was, the immaculate Sunset Boulevard side, it would be sure to go soon. Meanwhile we must all go down to the beach.

On the beach Clever Drawers kept saying to Sean, 'Why don't you sit down?'

'I am sitting down.'

'No you're not, you're squatting.'

'I am not.'

'Well – crouching then.'

'Yes, well I think I'll just take the kids for a little dip.'

An hour later Susie said, 'Is your tooth hurting Sean?'

'Not at the moment pet.'

'Well SIT DOWN then.'

'Well pet I don't think I will, just in case, you know how it is with sand, it gets everywhere, and anywhere, I mean it can get in places you hoped it wouldn't, and I've heard people say that it can be terrible, and coming from a medical family it has been made apparent to me, more than most, just how difficult it can be to get sand out of places where you would rather it wasn't, and I don't want to do anything rash that I might regret in view of the fact that sand can be a terrific problem in er – certain areas.'

Nothing would persuade Sean to sit, and although we all assured him that the moment we saw a grain of sand anywhere near him we would give the alarm – he couldn't be convinced. As he said, if something's ingrained into you, it's very difficult to get it out, and as Susie said there wasn't much point in being on the beach when one of you was CROUCHING – so we all went back to the club.

Even there – with no sand – it was difficult to feel relaxed, as it can be when you are aware that a man in a cotton hat is concentrating on you from afar. Just as it's difficult to get in and out of swimming pools without getting any water over the side. Not only that, but there was a cloud in the sky, and that's the sort of thing that can get you down when you're trying not to splash.

Back at the villa that evening we realized that the lavatories weren't working. Not only that, but there was beginning to be a smell which was strongly reminiscent of lavatories not working. Should we Ask The Man In The Cotton Hat For Help as Señor Smeeth had told us to do? Would Asking For A Plumber Constitute Victory? Should We Lure Him to the Villa and Suffocate Him with the Smell? Where was The Immaculate Maid? We wrestled through several bottles of wine as we pondered these and other questions.

Eventually we decided to lure Cotton Hat to the villa and

suffocate him with the smell. We could then enquire tenderly about a doctor for Sean's tooth, which was still making itself felt, and demand the home address of the immaculate maid who would be summoned immediately to take charge of the children who were beginning to fall out in spite of a mutual devotion to plastic knickers.

Clever Drawers and Sean went in search of Cotton Hat, while Susie and I separated the children into different rooms, and moved one of the double beds into the living room. It was obvious that until the maid arrived the off-spring would have to be kept in different cages, and as for Clever Drawers and I sleeping in the living room, we felt it could only be an improvement after being opposite the lavatories.

A certain amount of time elapsed before Sean and Clever Drawers returned accompanied not by Cotton Hat, but by one of his Spanish assistants. He sniffed the air judiciously, and then held his nose.

'Malo,' he said prophetically.

'Mucho malo wouldn't you say?'

'Mucho malo,' he agreed unmovingly.

'We must have el plumber.' We watched in admiration as Sean gesticulated dramatically with the hand that was not holding his tooth.

'Si.'

'El doctore – '

'Si.'

'El domestico.'

'Si.'

A sigh of relief went round the room. Here was a good fellow, a sympathetic fellow, a fellow who would go out of his way to pull his finger out on our behalf. The memory of Señor Smith's description of the friendly willing natives reaching out to help visitors from foreign shores came flooding back. What a good thing we had decided to act straight away. Very soon we would have flushing lavatories, smiling children, and Sean free of his toothache.

The future seemed so rosy that we thought it wise to have a celebration dinner down at that nice café. We would take the children, just like all the Continentals did, and we would dine and wine in readiness for tomorrow. A couple of hours later with plates in front of us piled high with unfinished food, Clever Drawers looked at the change in his hand. 'They've done us,' he said.

'What do you mean they've done us. Here give me the bill.' Sean stared at it, and five minutes went by as he counted up very slowly on his one free hand. 'They've done us.'

'They've overcharged us.'

'I'm sure it's not by very much,' I said hopefully, because I could see that the waiter, though small, was not small enough.

'What do you mean "not very much"? Do you realize they've charged us thirty shillings a head for that rubbish?'

'No, no, not thirty shillings,' Sean snatched the bill back. 'Look, if four and three is seven — ' There was another silence as he again added up with his one hand. Eventually he looked up, 'Do you realize they've charged us thirty shillings a head for that rubbish?'

'Exactly.'

'Oh no they don't.'

'Quite.'

'Not on your life.'

They advanced towards Mrs Paella who was sitting on a stool at the back of the room. For a few minutes there was the sound of voices raised in self-defence, and hands waving to and from a small blackboard where the prices were chalked up.

'Right.'

'That's the last time we come here.'

'What did they say?'

'They said those pieces of cottonwool were salmon.'

'I said if that's salmon then it must have been spawned in the Serpentine.'

We went back to the villa but only went to bed after we had tipped the remains of the Bourbon down Sean in the hope that he would be able to sleep. Clever Drawers and I lay like two washed up bottles in the middle of the living room. It was nice not being opposite the lavatories, but it was difficult to sleep because there was a strong wind which blew the deck chairs on the verandah backwards and forwards. All night. Relentlessly. Without ceasing.

In the morning Clever Drawers sat on the edge of the bed and looked at his feet. He had just been to the window and it was raining. We could hear the children hitting each other. I went into the kitchen. Sean was sitting at the table holding his jaw, his face pale as a paper bag. I went back into the sitting room where Clever Drawers was sitting. A doctor must be found, now, immediately. We drank our coffee and watched the rain trickling down the windows. We must find a doctor.

'El doctore?'

'Si, si,' the little boy ran ahead of us and pointed down the street.

'El doctore?'

'Si, si.' The woman held the door open for us and smiled.

'El doctore?'

'Si, si,' he removed the cigarette from his mouth, and a little of the ash trickled down his waistcoat.

'Mon amigo malo ici.' Clever Drawers pointed towards Sean's jaw.

'Si?'

'Si.'

'Malo?'

'Si, Malo.'

'Ah,' he smiled kindly at Sean and peered into his mouth. His eyes widened as they inspected the scene. He straightened up, took a long drag on his cigarette, and looked at Clever Drawers. 'Malo, malo,' he said, pointing to the right hand side.

'No, no, malo ici,' said Clever Drawers pointing to the left hand side.

'No, no,' the doctor shook his head, 'malo ici,' he pointed again to the right hand side.

'No, no, malo ici,' Clever Drawers opened Sean's mouth and pointed to the left hand side.

'No, no,' the doctor gesticulated impatiently, 'malo, MALO,' he lifted Sean's lip and tapped the four black stumps where the bridge had broken, 'malo – gangreno.'

'No – malo, no gangreno, bueno ici bueno,' Clever Drawers

186

too tapped the black stumps. 'Ici malo,' he lifted the other side of Sean's lip and gesticulated towards the Sunset Boulevard snowy white caps.

The doctor lit another cigarette, 'Non comprendez.' He shook his head, 'Malo?'

'Si.'

'Ici?'

'Non.'

'Non?'

'Non.'

'Non, malo ici?'

'Non.'

'Non gangreno?'

'Non gangreno.'

'Malo ICI?'

'Si.'

The doctor lowered Sean's lip, and shook his head. He stood looking at Sean for a minute hopeful that he might perhaps change his mind, and then he went to his desk and sat down heavily. Very carefully brushing the ash from it, he penned a prescription, then he beckoned Clever Drawers.

'Amigo?'

'Si.'

'Amigo – ' he pointed to the prescription 'uno – ' he waved three fingers, 'uno – '

'One every three hours.'

'Si.'

'Ma – non – ha, ha, hey, hey.' He mimed drinking.

Emerging into the hot street again we walked slowly back towards the town. Now for a chemist, and a telephone. It was Sean's idea. He would telephone London, speak to the dentist, see what he had to say, and follow his instructions. Simple.

The chemist was shut, so we made our way to the Post Office. A fat brown lady sat in front of a switchboard. She smiled plumply, and we passed the time of day in an exchange of 'mucho hot' and 'Si, si', eventually arriving at the purpose of our visit.

'Telephonez,' we said brightly pointing towards her switch-board.

'Si,' she smiled fanning herself. 'Telephone.'

'Telephonez Londres?'

'Si?'

'Telephonez Londres.'

'Ah telephonez Londres.'

'Si telephonez Londres.'

'Give her the number.'

'Barcelona – Londres.'

'She means you've got to phone Barcelona, then Londres.'

'Ah.'

We sat against the wall and fanned ourselves with our hats. The children played on the floor, and we watched with interest while the telephonist wound up the switchboard. Her windings were occasionally broken by muttering and gesticulation. She gesticulated at the buttons in front of her, and she muttered towards a beaded curtain, which sporadically answered her.

Eventually she turned towards us. 'Non – Barcelona – non.'

'What does she mean Barcelona non?'

'What do you think she means – Barcelona si?'

'Barcelona non? Pourque Barcelona non?' She fanned herself and shrugged. 'Barcelona non.' She looked sadly at the machine and sighed. There was a movement from behind the beaded curtain and an old lady appeared. She let out a stream of words at the machine, and kicked it. Again the telephonist wound it up, again the old lady kicked it, and then after a few more attempts she turned and shook her head sadly at us.

'Barcelona non?'

'Si, Barcelona non.' She retired back behind her beaded curtain.

'Mañana Barcelona?'

'Ah, si, mañana Barcelona.' But her voice held out little hope.

We collected Sean's pills from the chemist, and returned to the villa to find the maid waiting. She looked us up and down very carefully before deciding to cross the threshold.

'Hey – what's Spanish for children?' Clever Drawers shouted gleefully leading her into the sitting room.

'Will you look after the prole? Prole avec vous?'

'No.'

'Non?'

'No.'

'Señor Smith say si.'

'Señor Smeeth loco,' she tapped her head.

'Ah well, perhaps she'll do some cleaning.'

The next morning Scan was worse. Crumpled, white and silent. We decided we must find a dentist. Of course, how ridiculous, you don't go to a doctor with toothache – you go to the dentist. What would a doctor know about teeth? This time we would get it all sorted out once and for all and no 'malo icis' and 'buenos la' either, we would prepare ourselves in such a way that there would be no doubt as to where the pain was. With the help of a pocket dictionary I wrote out:

'Caro Dentista, Mon amigo tenc uno malo diente. Il diente no los dientes que sono negro, ma los dientes que sono blanco. Socorro – gracia.' Clever Drawers drew a diagram of Sean's mouth, colouring in the relevant teeth, and displaying the place where the pain was.

The dentist lived thirty miles away. We were gratified to see a number of other people holding their jaws in the waiting room.

'She says he'll be free at eleven o'clock.'

Some time was spent trying to read the back of the *Barcelona Echo*, before it was time for Sean to go in. At the sight of the spotless surgery filled with magnificent equipment even he brightened. It was obvious we had at last come to the right place. The dentist shook each of our hands in turn before reading my note. I had added at the bottom at Clever Drawers' suggestion 'P.S. Mon amigo a una diagramma por expliqar.'

'Comprende?'

'Si.'

'Give him the diagram.'

He stared at it, and then he looked from it to Clever Drawers, and from Clever Drawers back to the diagram. He shook his head very slowly then he smiled and wrung his hand several times. 'Amigo – magnifico. Magnifico.'

'Sorry?'

'He likes your diagram – he thinks it's magnifico.'

'Thank you very much.'

'No – amigo – magnifico, magnifico.'

'Do you really think so?'

'Si, si.'

'Oh I don't know – '

'Comprende diagrama?'

'Si, si, magnifico.'

Still smiling he opened Sean's mouth. Very slowly he inspected one side, and then the other, and then he put his hand in his pocket and took out his cigarettes. He beckoned to Clever Drawers. 'Amigo – ' he tapped the side of his own face 'Amigo – malo – malo.'

'Si, si, malo malo.'

He lowered his voice, 'Amigo – gangreno.'

'Non!'

'No?'

'Non. Amigo non gangreno, amigo malo, non gangreno.'

'Si, si.'

'Non, non.'

'Here we go again.'

'Read him your note again.'

'Show him the diagram.'

'No read him the note.'

' "Caro Dentista – " '

'That's right read him the note.'

'Mon amigo tene uno malo diente.'

'Si.'

'Il diente – no los que sono NEGRO.'

'No?'

'Non. Ma los dientes que sono BLANCO.'

'Ah?'

'Si, que sono BLANCO.'

The dentist very slowly re-approached Sean, his cigarette bent with ash, and re-opened his mouth. His eyes swivelled from one side of the mouth to the other.

'Negro – no malo?'

'Non.'

'Blanco malo?'

'Si.'

He shook his head gloomily several times. When he spoke it was at some speed and volubility.

'I think he's trying to tell us something.'

'Non comprende. Êtes-vous Frances speaking?'

'Ask the nurse.'

'Êtes-vous Frances speaking?'

'Si.'

'What's he saying?'

'She says he's saying he can't do anything about it.'

'What do you mean he can't do anything about it?'

'He says the tooth needs X-raying?'

'What's this equipment for – cleaning his car?'

'She says he's only qualified to do extractions.'

'Dear heavens.'

We realized that there was nothing more we could do. The instruction leaflet was still hanging from the X-ray machine, but it was in German. Sean would have to go back to England. If he got better – they would fly out again. Two hours later we drove away from the airport. We were on our own now, and the lavatories were still not working.

In the morning we decided we would not be Got Down. We would assume a jollity we did not feel. We put on the gramophone while we ate breakfast. 'All you need is . . . Who Ho Ho . . . Who Ho . . . Ho-o' the batteries were running out, and all we really needed was a plumber.

Needing a plumber is a good way to re-assess your life. Until you need a plumber you might hitherto have not had the respect you should have for gentlemen employed in the plumbing trade. You might have dismissed a plumber as being a person who does a job like anyone else. You might have taken plumbers for granted – like telephones. 'Let's telephone a plumber' is a sentence that takes on added dimensions when you are half way up a mountain, and the lavatories aren't working.

We spent the morning on the beach, and then we drove towards the club. There was no one anywhere, it being siesta hour, but our need for a plumber was greater than sanity. We would demand a plumber, we would invoke the U.N. Charter, we would shout Nation Shall Send Plumbers Unto Nation. Cotton Hat would be forced to supply our needs before the state of our villa became an International Incident. Suddenly a smell of burning rubber filled the car.

'The clutch is burnt out.'

'What?'

'The clutch is burnt out.'

'What do we do now?'

'Wait until someone drives by.'

We pushed the car into the shade and waited. The heat hung like a velvet curtain round us. We didn't talk in case the effort drained away some necessary ounce of liquid which would later prove to be irreplaceable. Eventually we heard the hum of a truck. He passed us, then stopped some yards up the hill. We ran to him, and clutched the side of his van in case it was a mirage.

'You speakez Frances un peu?'

'Oui, oui.'

'He was brought up in Algeria.'

'Well what's the Algerian for clutch?'

Watching this god-like man bending over the engine it seemed as if the phoenix was in the ascendant again. He looked so pretty, so neat, it wasn't possible that he was human with his cool shades and his immaculate shorts. Not only that, he was a genuine mechanic. A man qualified to mend cars, a man who knew his dip stick from his throttle, who could locate a cylinder head with his eyes shut. Bess you is my woman now.

Our admiration knew no bounds when he produced a tow rope and drove us slowly and carefully into town. It was quite obvious that Algeria was a breeding ground for genius. He was not only prepared to mend the car – he told us where to find a plumber, and himself offered to escort us to the house of the plumber.

At The House of The Plumber. I could find no provision made for such exigencies in my phrase book. The usual 'this has got a hole in it' and 'do you want it wrapped?' but nothing about ess bends or ball cocks. Making a mental note to write to the publishers on this score, we made do with mime. I pulled Clever

Drawers' chain a few times, and he came up with some useful sounds, and of course holding our noses and a general chorus of 'malos' conveyed the extreme urgency of the situation.

The plumber, although not brought up in Algeria, was a cousin of the mechanic, and it was not long before he agreed to accompany us to the villa, while the mechanic promised to mend the clutch within the next few days. Things were looking up, positively euphoric in fact.

We opened all doors and windows, and the plumber set to work. Two hours later we all shook hands. An International Incident had been averted. We shook hands yet again. It became apparent that he would not be averse to sampling some alcohol.

He was still with us when darkness fell.

'Barcelona very beautiful.'

'Si, si.'

'Madrid very beautiful.'

'Si, si.'

Two faces appeared at the edge of the balcony.

'Heavens they gave me el fright.'

The faces belonged to the local police – the Guardia Civil. They too were obviously not strangers to plumbing difficulties – they shook hands warmly with our friend. Then after much back-slapping he decided it was time to go home, and as he went, pocketing two or three notes, the Guardia Civil settled themselves into the wicker chairs.

It is sometimes difficult to know what to do with two armed men when they have settled themselves into your wicker chairs. To point out that they are superfluous to your entertainment might be tactless, and talking is a strain when you have already spent a number of hours communicating your delight at the beauty of Barcelona and environs. Clever Drawers' eye lighted on the games box. The international passport to communication. Poker could be weighted rather heavily in favour of their rifles, so he chose Pick-A-Sticks.

In a remarkably short time they had learnt how to spill their sticks, and hold their breath while removing each stick without touching another. Shirt collars were unbuttoned, and drinks poured out, as they bent over the table mesmerized. During the

13

interval I indicated their rifles. What did nice men like them want horrid guns like that for I wondered?

'Bandidos – bang bang.'

'Oh bandidos – bang bang. Of course. How silly of me.'

'I shouldn't think they're even loaded.' Clever Drawers had once won a cup for the cleanest rifle, so he obviously knew what he was talking about. As for bandidos – that was obviously Spanish for grouse, or pigeon. Bandido pie – very tasty.

Halfway through the second intense bout of pick-a-sticking, the still air was fractured by a slight rustle, a miniature noise, a small sound; within seconds the pick-a-sticks lay at our feet, and our acquaintances were vaulting the verandah. There was a burst of intense fire, and then a silence. We peered cautiously over the rails. Below us they were re-shouldering their guns. Beside them a pile of white things lay riddled with bullets. Susie's disposable nappies were now dead.

'*Adios.*'

'*Mañana.*'

'*Si, mañana.*'

We settled down to sleep in the middle of the ocean of broken furniture that made up the sitting room. It obviously didn't do to be a floating nappy in Spain. Not only that but being white, fluttering, and on a hill could mean that you'd have a slight aertex effect to you by the next morning. The trouble with seeing dead nappies is that it can suddenly remind you that you're the only people occupying a villa for miles around. It can suddenly communicate to you that being on your own on a hill, above the sea is one thing, but being on your own on a hill, above the sea, without a telephone, is quite another, particularly when it comes to dialling nueve, nueve, nueve.

Over the next few days we tried to break up the monotony of our existence by celebrating such events as the Return of the Car, the day the Maid did the Ironing, and Meeting an English Couple, but even so they formed themselves into a pattern.

'Get Up. Breakfast to old forty-five records played at thirty and a half revolutions. Read old Raymond Chandlers found under bed. Go to beach. Lunch. Siesta. Go to Club. Talk to English couple. Play pick-a-sticks with Guardia. Go to Sleep.'

We used to look forward to seeing the English couple. It was one of the highlights of our day. Too soon it was time for them to go. We envied them, feeling like prisoners serving a longer sentence. They bought us drinks to celebrate their return. Good old England. They were going to kiss their telephone when they got back. Wasn't it funny how much you appreciated it once you didn't have it? Yes, wasn't it? It must be awful stuck up on that hill. Yes, it was pretty lonely. Mind you, they'd got rid of most of the bandits.

What did she mean most of the bandits? I drained my fifth absinth and stared distractedly at my foot. I am a fully practising devout coward. If I could have crawled to Clever Drawers on my hands and knees and begged him not to return us to the villa I would have done, but I no longer knew where my hands and feet were. I could not even communicate to him in sentences containing separate words, everything kept coming out like Constantinople. My foot had assumed what I can only describe as proportions – proportions as large as the 'most' that had hovered in her sentence. Inwardly, inside my brain, where I knew I was still functioning, I thought – 'At least *most* of the bandits" wasn't "*a few* of the bandits" – ' Then I thought 'Does "most of the bandits" assume you know that there are quite a few left? If so how many? And what size?' Perhaps I had missed hearing her say – "There are only a *couple of* most of the bandits left." '

When we got back to the villa it was dark and the dim lights and the small furniture did nothing to make it more welcoming. The air outside was thick, thick with Most of the Bandits I could see peopling the hill behind us. Memories of a picture in an old French exercise book came back to me. I remembered bandits were large, black-haired individuals who came at you with knives in their teeth. La plume de ma tante. When the first flash of lightning struck, it was a relief. That would put them off. Not even bandits would come at you during a storm. We locked ourselves in our room with a meat cleaver.

After that it was nothing but steady progress downhill, with the day of departure being the upward trend. The Guardia Civil no longer called in the evenings. Whether their addiction to pick-a-sticks had been reported to a superior more Guardia than Civil we didn't know, but now when they passed us on their motor bikes during the day, they did no more than raise a hand in greeting, and motor on.

The day of departure was a good day. We kicked each stick of furniture by turn, and we piled our suitcases into the car and slammed the villa door shut. We were off – never to return again. Adios bandidos, adios villa, adios café. As we turned the corner all that we could see up on the hill beside the white of the villa, was a smaller blob of white. The remaining packets of Susie's disposable nappies.

8

It's surprising how often things work out for better or for worse according to how you look at it. I mean the moment when you realize that your book about the Chinese invading Ireland has turned out to be a waste of time, is a moment which some might loosely describe as melancholy. On the other hand it could be time to celebrate, because there is a strong chance you will realize, from that moment on, that the subject has not got the potential you once thought. 'You only learn the hard way' happens to be one of Worcester's favourite expressions, the trouble is she usually says it when you just have.

These thoughts and others like it went through my mind as I lay on the airport bench with Clever Drawers the night we missed the plane in our haste to get out of Spain. On the one hand it could be argued that people who got the time of the plane wrong – in spite of a Higher Education – were incompetent. On the other hand – with reference to Worcester's motto – it could be argued that he would never again mistake twenty-two twenty for twenty past eleven.

Similarly sleeping the night at an airport teaches you that charter flights leave more often than you think for Gatwick and Manchester, and they are not good news when it comes to being able to give people lifts, just as airport benches are not designed for people who have vertebrae. It also teaches you that airport officials are quick to see the profits to be made from travellers in distress, and at such times it is good to be travelling with a man whose ancestors trod the soil of Yorkshire because they tend to be quick to see the officials trying to make a profit.

When we did at last sight our front door again, the knowledge that it was no longer ours was distinctly lowering. I mean to return bronzed and fit, ready to be on the credits had been our

197

ambition – in the light of which selling the house hadn't much relevance, but when the tan has turned to fawn, and the credits are not forthcoming – fit takes on a new meaning. Dot, dot, dot.

Something must be done, we thought with startling originality. Sitting about the house realizing that only our tummies were now brown was not exactly constructive. Any more than spending hours in the supermarket sticking out your tongue at the closed circuit television. We had to find a way, the way, some way. Some months were spent thinking along these lines until we decided we would definitely become playwrights, together. After all we were both there, and if you're both there you might as well do something about it.

Becoming playwrights together isn't as easy as it sounds. Living with someone is easier than working with them. I mean, in certain circumstances I would rather live with a lot of people than work with them. Of course I'd rather not do either, but if I-had-fallen-into-the-hands-of-the-enemy-and-had-to-save-someone's-life – and they were good enough to give you a choice, I think I'd rather shut my eyes and think of England, than work with them.

Working with someone can be very embarrassing. In fact there can be fewer more toe curling experiences than to watch someone's expression the other side of a desk turning from disbelief to horror at the inanity of your suggestions. Even once over that hurdle there are the silences to deal with. Silences where you are both hoping that the other person is thinking along straighter lines than you are. Silences where my mind tends to turn towards how many beans make five, and we can't have stew again tonight. Then after the silences there's the problem of staring at each other. The sudden discovery of a mole on the other person's face that you imagine you haven't glimpsed before. The realization that your hair is *exactly* the same colour, and you have *exactly* the same habit of scratching your eyebrows. Exclamation mark.

It isn't until you work with someone else that you discover that you have a lot of habits, most of them bad. You like reading the back of gas bills, and making lists, and you stick pencils in your ears when you get stuck. He on the other hand is addicted to flicking through motoring magazines, drawing arrows all over the desk, and dunking his biscuits. However, if things progress, it isn't many months before you are both sticking pencils in your ears, and dunking your biscuits.

We definitely got the idea that things were progressing after our first half dozen plays. Unfortunately no one else seemed to be so definite about it. Little things convey this to you. Scripts sent back with tea stains and chair marks on them. Readers' letters – 'there is nothing, and no one, of interest in this play'. The doors were closed. The buildings had no windows.

In the end you give up, and go back to wondering whether to be Clark Gable after all. You realize you could fill your whole house with plays, and never sell one. You estimate the cost in paper alone if you go on writing and not selling, and it works out that you can't afford the paper or the carbon let alone the typing ribbon. You realize you are providing free doorstops, beer mats, and desk props for organizations all over London, and it goes against the grain.

After a little while you even forget that you were meant to be going to be brilliant, and you take to earning your living in other ways. You put up with friends who tell you you've sold out, who shake their heads and hold you up as examples of bourgeois beastliness. There are very good reasons for not wanting to write plays, and it isn't long before you've found most of them.

Then someone picks up the telephone, and starts the whole thing off again. The whole hopeless flick through the notebook for ideas that could sound all right. If only people wouldn't ask such stupid questions. Imagine asking if you had any ideas? Imagine actually phoning up and asking you if you had any ideas? Of course you've got ideas, just because you can't remember what they are doesn't mean to say you haven't got them.

Of course there are various aids to concentration when going for an interview. Imagining someone without their clothes on is statutory but effective, particularly when you have just fallen off your chair or, like Clever Drawers, set light to their cushions.

Still, it is much better when there are two of you, and only one of him. You can feel superior, if only in numbers. You can exchange a look at various telling points which can make him

Hasten to Add Something. Hastening to Add is letting the enemy see the whites of your eyes. Once you have got someone Hastening to Add, you can start walking about his office and rearranging his furniture. You can put your chewing gum in his ashtray, and sort through his wastepaper basket. Hastening to Add is the sign to look for.

Actually there's always been a sort of rift between Clever Drawers and me as regards Conduct at an Interview. I mean I've always believed in bending the truth, highlighting the might have beens as it were, whereas he is a Truth Is Better Than Fiction person. He can't seem to understand that people aren't interested in the truth. He has this fantastic idea that people want to employ you for what you are, instead of what they hope you are.

Our progress to the interview was marked by a general tendency to yawn, clear our throats, and dart in and out of conveniences. There's a feel about a now or never interview – it has a marked similarity to thinking you've got the 'flu. Particularly when you've arrived at the door and the secretary is looking at you, making you feel glad you've got your good coats on, and at the same time feeling sorry they're not a bit gooder.

Coats have an extraordinary importance at interviews – even when you get inside the inner sanctum and you've shaken hands with the great man, the problem of what to do with them can haunt you. If you keep them on, it can make it look as if you don't think he's worth staying for, and what's more his office is cold. On the other hand, if you take them off, you may panic him into thinking you're never going to leave.

We took them off. Clever Drawers looked at me. I had forgotten to sew the lining of mine, and all the buttons were hanging off. On the great man's desk lay a piece of paper from our past. It gleamed with last year's enthusiasm. He picked it up, and my mind immediately started to wander as it usually does when people start discussing plays you haven't yet written, and possibly might not. I came back when the great man was in the middle of wondering whether or not we'd be interested in a commission, and Clever Drawers was in the middle of wondering whether we could spare the time. It wasn't that we weren't interested, I was glad to hear, it was just that there were so many pressures. I chewed my gum in a pressurized sort of way.

Half an hour later we walked out into the sunshine. We were commissioned. Don't walk on the lines. Set 'em up Joe. We were going to write a play and someone was going to pay us money for it. The buildings had windows again.

9

I don't know how we got invited down to Lord and Lady Thyng's. I mean I know how we got invited, but not why. It's not what I call usual in the history of our relationship to pass the week-end doing anything more than quarrelling about who should make the gravy.

The trouble with those sort of invitations is that you usually accept them. Naturally you give yourself good grounds for so doing. If you never Get Out, you tell each other, how will you ever Find Out? And then again, we all know what happens to people who don't go anywhere, in the end they never get anywhere. And what's more, you add perceptively, the good thing about staying with people like Thyng is that you don't have to do the washing up, and that is a very good thing.

Now, of course, I tell myself that if we hadn't been up to here with everything, we probably would not have felt this unusual urge both to accept an invitation, and deposit ourselves at a house party. But when you've just had your first play performed you are in an enfeebled state, you are weakened, you are not what you were, if you know what I mean.

In fact, the play was the cause of our being invited. Thyng had felt a wild urge to contact his old friend from University when he had viewed it. He had flung himself on the hot line at once, demanding our presence at his gathering. Apparently it would not be what it should be, unless we were there. If we did not turn up, he – and others – would be in danger of not enjoying themselves. The Upper Echelons needed us.

When we were sorting through our wardrobe some hours later, we came to the conclusion that there wasn't much you could do when people exerted such pressure. As we tried to breathe life back into various faded garments, we imagined the sheer responsibility of not going. The discomfort of knowing that we had ruined the festivities down at Thyng's place, that we were solely responsible for a patch of boredom appearing at Thyng Abbey in the County of Wiltshire. It was a responsibility that we were not prepared to shoulder, so we set off down the King's Road in search of clothes suitable for attending house parties.

The schedule of entertainment had not been mentioned, but we imagined part of the Festivities would include activities such as falling down rabbit holes, and off horses, all of which pastimes required being clothed. We were determined to fall down rabbit holes in garments which could be judged to be mildly acceptable. Unfortunately, the King's Road did not offer completely the right thing. It's very difficult to age a tweed suit up to the exact level of faded shabbiness overnight, just as it takes a lot of the right wear and tear to make a hat look as if it knows your head well. There is nothing worse than knowing that your hat feels embarrassed.

After a great deal of speculation we committed ourselves to among other things a green tweed suit, some purple socks, a number of hats, and some shortie pyjamas, which though not suitable for falling down rabbit holes, we were confident had enough appeal to please the most particular maid. We felt that each evening she would lay them out with the kind of enjoyment that springs from the knowledge that Thyng's guests were people who knew what was what when it came to night attire.

The day we were due to drive down to Thyng Abbey, we were still hoping we might be lucky enough to get a chill. The prospect of spending nearly a week passing the port and joining the ladies was not doing Clever Drawers very much good. He kept saying things like. 'There'll probably be a lot of Old Etonians there.' He doesn't like Etonians – not since they threw buns at his school motto. It's the sort of thing a chap remembers unkindly.

Still, we packed up the tweeds and the sensible shoes, and the evening suit, ready to set off in our highly polished car, because that's the sort of sincerity we have. We are not the sort of people who arrive in a mud caked Bugatti and toss the steering wheel to the groom with instructions to clean it. We spend hours polishing hub caps and retrieving chewing gum papers from under the seats, so that nobody will offer to clean it, and we will be spared the strain of trying to decide whether to tip them, or send them a nice postcard next time we go on holiday.

Clever Drawers had been a bit vague as to what Thyng was like. His descriptions varied from his being the sort of person who was always found under the table at Boat Club dinners but red-hot for every girl in College, to being 'quite a good crack when he forgot the English thing'. I imagined a man with hot eyes, a slight slur to his speech, and a torn Etonian tie.

'Charlie. My dear fellow.'

'John.'

We stood in the hall. It was large. Two Irish Wolf-hounds sloped towards us. Thyng was not at all what I had imagined, because although wearing tweed, it was confined only to his legs, while the rest of him was a noble attempt at minor Maharishi-dom. He sported an Indian scarf, and although he hadn't been able to grow what was left of his hair, he had succeeded rather better around his face, which displayed a long moustache, so long in fact that it looked false, and gave you the impression that you had caught him in the middle of dressing up. He was a miracle of conflicting ideologies.

Our bedroom was large with highly mattressed beds. From the window you could see hills and a waterfall. We unpacked, and set up the refreshment bar, something which is always a feature when staying away. A few packets of biscuits and a fruit cake are a necessity against the panic that can set in when you realize that you are not going to be given a square meal. It has not been unknown for some people's house guests to collide in the supermarket while intent on stocking up in order to hold out until the end of their stay. Just as at certain black spots round the English countryside, the weakness of the host's pouring arm can produce a crop of people who keep having to go up to their rooms to see if their bedroom slippers are still all right.

Dressing was a lonely business as Clever Drawers' clothes had been laid out in a room next door. Struggling on my own with a zip led me to think that being a rich man's plaything might not be as much fun as one once imagined. The lack of communal life could get you down, him dressing in one place, and you in another, and then meeting downstairs as if you were in a play. Of course, it all depends on what you are used to. On what you see yourselves as.

We thought we looked all right when we met in the middle of the room. Formal, but with just a touch of dash – like a pink gin. Clever Drawers sported his purple socks, in spite of the fact that his black ones had been laid out by way of a hint. I had remembered to brush my hair, so the scene was nicely set.

Thyng's pouring arm was well up to standard, and he had a good selection. It raises the hopes to see a good selection well laid out. It makes one feel easy in one's mind, relaxed in one's attitude. One can take it or leave it at will when it's all there, whereas the terror that sets in when faced with an inadequate display can turn the lightest drinker into a violent alcoholic. It can make Grannies into drunkards to see only a bottle of Elderberry wine and a half-empty tonic jostling uneasily on a drink tray.

Thyng was inclined to dart. He was tall, but darting came easily to him. He conversed while breaking the lap record between gramophone and drinks. It was cold when you stood away from the fire, and the draught from under the doors curled his moustache upwards, but he was unaware of it – which was a good thing since he wore only a cotton vest with his evening trousers.

'We've got some Pop staying, did you know?' said Thyng.

'Really?'

Clever Drawers' face brightened, and I tried to forget that we had just bought him a tweed suit more suitable for falling down rabbit holes than chatting Pop up.

The next two guests were definitely not Pop, thank goodness. We were not going to be entirely alone in our un-gear. Mr and Mrs Moulded Chiffon had made for tradition as well. She had sticking out teeth such as you are rarely privileged to see, and he had small eyes which narrowed even further as he watched Thyng raise the gin bottle.

'Knew a chap who could pour a double straight on the mark,'

he said. 'Straight on the mark. You've got lipstick on your teeth, Diana.'

'Oh heavens.'

'Always getting lipstick on her teeth,' he told me. 'Had it on when I first met her.'

The next person down was Lady Thyng accompanied by an actress named Kate. They walked into the room looking like a before and after advertisement. Depending on what you thought was what, you could before or after either of them. Lady Thyng – who was referred to by everybody as 'Lady' – was completely untouched by time. She had on a dinner frock with matching shoes, and her blonde hair was coiffured. Her friend, on the other hand, was as loose as she was kempt. She flowed in different directions, and when she sat down we were privileged to see that the soles of her feet were hard and black.

'Such fun,' murmured Mrs Moulded Chiffon, and I could see that her teeth had moved out even further in her effort to take it all in.

Next to amble in was Julian Fashist-Pigge. The Moulded Chiffons' faces brightened on catching sight of him.

'Ju-Ju!' they cried in unison, making his appearance an opportunity to palm another double.

Ju-Ju was full of fun. He rumbled towards them uttering noises. He squeezed various hands. His bow tie was very small and he twinkled fatly above it. As he reached out for his whisky and soda he said:

'I see we have Miss Unmade-Bed with us.'

The Moulded Chiffons laughed delightedly. He was such a card. Not only that, but he must be so tired after all those hours spent sitting in the House of Commons.

'Kate. Would you like a drink?' asked Lady Thyng.

'No thanks Lady, I'm smoking.'

The actress's eyes rolled towards the door and the entrance of her boy-friend, accompanied by the Pop.

Sammy Denim had his arms around their shoulders. He pushed them forward. They both had long golden glossy hair, and velvet suits.

'What sort of thing would you like?' asked Thyng kindly in the silence that followed, as the Moulded Chiffons and Ju-Ju bulged at the sight of them.

'Three orangeades,' said Sammy, on behalf of all of them. Then he added: 'We got some good stuff done this afternoon.'

'We're starting a pop group called The Thyng,' said Thyng to Clever Drawers. 'Rather good, don't you think?'

The Pop had retreated to a window seat where one of them was busy twisting his long golden hair round his fingers, while the other very seriously tipped peanuts into his mouth from a cut glass bowl.

'I can't get over how *unspoilt . . .* '

Sammy gestured towards the Pop.

'Yes. They are unspoilt.'

Thyng shook his head.

'Their *purity.*'

Sammy had a way of throwing a word up into the air, and when it crashed to the floor waiting for someone else to pick it up.

'Their purity,' echoed Thyng. 'Fantastic.'

'They are *fantastic.*'

'Amazing, Sammy.'

'Yes, really amazing.'

'I think it's time we went into dinner.'

The Moulded Chiffons' faces brightened considerably over dinner. The food and wine were first class. Lady Thyng smiled down the table at the Pop who were flicking water from their finger bowls. She said 'Such fun' several times, and Julian Fashist-Pigge wondered whether they would be leaving with the ladies?

'You'll have such a lot to talk about,' he insisted. 'Hairdressers, and frocks – and all that sort of thing.'

His level of wit was well up to Parliamentary standards.

Later, when the ladies withdrew to contemplate the coffee tray, it occurred to me that being a lady in the Upper Echelons is quite bad news. Women are not rated, or if they are, it's not as human beings. More as props. Catch a man talking to a woman and he looks shifty, as if he's afraid someone's going to come round the corner any minute and give him a bad mark. I've never understood whether it's because they don't actually like women, or whether it's because they have spent so much time of their adolescence locked up with each other, the sight of a woman gets them in a twist.

They're all right if they think you've done something. If they think you can read and write and might have one or two things worked out, they will force themselves to converse with you. But even then you get the feeling they've just switched on an egg timer.

It isn't until you actually dine with them however, that you realize to what extent they will go to avoid women. Not content with having clubs where women have to crawl up the back stairs in order to have a drink, where there are special pieces of carpet that women's feet must not be allowed to desecrate, they can't even bear to have the whole of dinner with them in their own homes. They spend a fortune on a social event, building it up, mixing people like *hors d'œuvre*, and filling them with food and wine, then just as everything's going nicely, they give the old lady a nod, and all the women leave the room so that the gentlemen can tell dirty stories, drink port and pee in the wine coolers. Some men even do it on their own. I mean, even when they're dining alone they make their wives leave them so that they can drink the port on their tod and tell themselves a dirty joke. 'Do stop me if I've told me this before.'

There's always a look of despair on Clever Drawers' face when he sees this is just about to happen, because he likes women. Not only that, but he likes talking to them as well. In fact he likes to talk to them more than he likes talking to men.

'It's amazing how long it takes people to roll a joint of grass, isn't it?'

Lady Thyng handed me my coffee cup.

'I always think it must be part of the fun,' she continued. 'Sitting there with the little bits of paper and the tobacco and so on. Otherwise why do they never get quicker at it?'

'Because they're always too high,' giggled Kate from the corner, where she was slaving over her joints. 'Like some grass?'

Mrs Moulded Chiffon stared at her disbelievingly.

'Not just for the moment, thank you,' she said. And then in case Lady Thyng was offended by her refusal, she murmured, 'The young are so original nowadays, aren't they?'

There were sounds of laughter from the dining room. It later appeared that Julian Fashist-Pigge had thrown a bread roll at one of the Pop. Half an hour later, the gentlemen joined the ladies.

Even later back in our room, Clever Drawers sighed, and looked at his socks for a few minutes, as he is prone to do when baffled.

'You should have been there,' he said thickly, and I handed him a piece of fruit cake, because it was very late, and elegant food always leaves a few gaps. 'He threw a bread roll. They don't change a bit, these Etonians. Absolute compulsion to throw bread at people.'

'Perhaps we ought to send ourselves a telegram?' I suggested helpfully. But we didn't, because on the next day there was a race meeting, and there's nothing like the sight of a few horses to put life in old Clever Drawers, even if it does mean going with an old Etonian or two.

The Pop were busily engaged on creative pursuits with Sammy the following day, so that the Moulded Chiffons, the Thyngs and ourselves were the only people to meet up at the races. Lady Thyng and Mrs Moulded Chiffon stood apart from the men, holding their race cards and pencils as if they expected them to be marked for the next dance. I joined the men at the bar. Their faces had assumed the seriousness of people who were discussing the one subject they knew really mattered. We were surrounded by ladies of immaculate stupidity who stood holding their gins to their noses. It was difficult to hear any of the tips that were being muttered above the cawing of the County voices.

'I always choose the one with the biggest bum,' said Mr Moulded Chiffon. 'And that goes for women too.'

'Hear Tom's got a good one in The Daily, you know.' Thyng looked at me significantly.

'Yes. I heard the same thing,' I agreed.

I didn't know who Tom was, nor why he should take time

out to own a horse called The Daily, but if anyone says things like that to me, I always assume they don't want me to disagree with them. Just as when people ask me if I know someone I always says yes. I mean, there's no point in saying no, because they're going to go on telling you their story anyway, so you might as well say yes, and save them the bother of telling you who it is that you don't know. If you know what I mean.

'That was a nasty business last year, nasty business. I felt very sorry for Tom.'

Thyng's smooth face puckered slightly under his brown hat. He was all of a piece today. Tweeds, brown hat, and the binocular strap bisecting the chest like the Order of the Garter.

'I didn't write to him. Did you?'

'No,' I replied. 'I thought it better not.'

'One can't very well put – "Sorry she's gone orf with the groom" in a letter now can one? Be a bit of a pantomime, wouldn't it?'

'Absolutely.'

Thyng's accent had assumed the natural constriction that is fascinating to listen to. 'Groom' had become 'grum' now we were away from the Pop. In certain moments of boredom it is well worth trying to play 'Spot The Lips Moving' when you go racing. We usually indulge while waiting for the horses to be led around the paddock. The County accent and the Cockney accent have, in many respects, a lot in common. Both are spoken from the back of the throat, both despise the use of the tongue against the roof of the mouth, and both drop their aitches.

' 'Ear shees married some fella oos vair well 'orf,' the lady behind me with the crocodile handbag and matching shoes had just remarked in phonetically perfect Cockney.

'My gardener – yer know me gardener – 'ee ses numbar eighteen,' said her friend.

'One up to me,' muttered Clever Drawers. 'She moved her bottom lip.'

'I say.' One of them tapped him sharply on the arm. 'Aren't you on the Wircless?'

'Not at the moment, no,' he replied. 'The crystal's gone again.'

'Oh. Oh isn't that 'strordinary, could have sworn one had seen you on the Wireless.'

She turned back to her friend as if she'd just dropped a wet tea towel.

'We don't watch it at all acherly,' said her companion. 'Nannia 'as the only set in the 'ouse.'

Thyng had invited us to watch the first race from the hush of the Jockey Club. You don't meet Jockeys in the Jockey Club, only owners in tweeds. I was glad Clever Drawers had come into his own at last. We stood next to an Old Gentleman with white hair. He said nothing. We said nothing. The horses swept past us the first time round. Binoculars moving was the only sign that anybody was actually alive. Then as The Daily and another equine specimen by the name of Grunt 'N Grumble fought their way to the finishing post, Clever Drawers let out a roar, which when loosely translated from the Gaelic meant 'Come on my son.' But too late, The Daily was beaten.

There was utter silence from all around us, as several pairs of fossilized eyes stonily regarded us. Were we going to be thrown out with the old watercress sandwiches? Black-balled from racing balconies throughout England? The Old Gentleman came to our rescue. He touched Clever Drawers on the arm.

'Bloody nearly shouted him home, didn't we?'

'Yes, we bloody nearly did,' Clever Drawers agreed.

'I like a bloody good shout,' said the Old Gentleman.

'So do I,' said Clever Drawers.

'That's the trouble with this damned place,' grumbled the Old Gentleman. 'Nobody shouts enough. All too busy stuffing sandwiches.'

We returned to Thyng Abbey in jovial form. We had had some winners. Picking winners is a very satisfactory business. Nothing can go wrong when you've had a few winners. Not only that, but you suddenly realize all sorts of things about yourself that you never realized before. Like the way your eye can take in a horse at twenty yards, and just like that tell you its potential. The way you have this natural instinct for them, this flair as it were. Not like after you've had a bad day when you will freely admit that you don't know one end of a thoroughbred from the

211

other, and that anyway everyone-knows-that-punting-is-a-mug's-game.

Above the table in the hall there was a large poster. There was going to be a party the following evening, and the theme was to be 'Revolution'. I looked round the hall with its large inlaid table, its air of vulnerable capitalism. How many parties had it witnessed in the past? How many drunken revels? I can go on like that for hours when I really feel like it.

'I suppose this party's going to be nothing but Hooray Henries.'

Clever Drawers looked at me gloomily from over the side of the bath. He is constantly presenting a smiling face to the world, while intent on filling me with Grave Doubts.

'Oh I don't know,' I said.

'Expect it will be full of Bloodies fresh from driving their motorbikes round Harrods.'

He has this dread of meeting Hooray Henries on motorbikes in the Banking Hall at Harrods.

'Oh I don't know,' I said again, but this time I said it through my second slice of fruit cake. 'Have another piece of cake,' I added, because there's nothing like a little snack to cheer a chap up when he's feeling low.

The trouble with Clever Drawers is that he doesn't like parties. He likes Dinner, and chat, and all that sort of thing, but he doesn't like a Party. Rooms full of people making merry are inclined to get him down, and the arrival of an invitation asking him somewhere can bring on one of those very quick and unexpected trips to Ireland that can really surprise a person, coming right out of nowhere as they so often do.

I must say, I can't admit the idea of a party ever makes me see stars either. People always expect something out of you at a party, something extra, something you can't quite put your finger on, but you know you haven't got. You're meant to be different from normal at parties, full of hairstyle and joosh, and you're meant to dance and rush about, and I don't like dancing or rushing about. And anyway, the only time I ever tried it, I caused a disturbance by falling over on the dance floor, and a scandal because I kept dancing with the same person on account of the fact that I was under the illusion that they were different people. Which is another reason why I believe in a good healthy snack before being forced to go 'What Ho' and 'Oh my deah how fascinating'. If the tummy is full, there is going to be far less chance of you falling over and causing a scandal.

Then there's another problem. The 'How Far Can I go?' Problem. This is something that no one has so far solved. Basically there are two choices open to a person at a party. Either you laugh and go 'Oh my deah how fascinating' and invite the sort of invitations that are not found on mantelpieces, or you spend some six or seven hours contemplating the canapés and earning a reputation of unrelieved boredom. No doubt the latter would be my lot the following evening. In the meanwhile, there was another dinner, and another breakfast to get through.

'Thank heavens when a fellow goes shootin' and talks about grass, at least he means the stuff you walk through.'

Mr Moulded Chiffon banged his coffee cup down, and prepared to leave the dining room as one of the Pop floated in.

'Wait for me, man,' said Sammy Denim, looking up from his newspaper. 'I want to come too, man.'

'I am quite well aware of what sex I am.' Mr Moulded Chiffon glared at him. 'But I am not aware of why you should want to shoot.'

'Listen. It's this whole life and death thing, man – ' Sammy got up and sauntered out with him. 'This whole life and death thing.'

'Yes but dammit what bore do you use?'

The door closed behind them. No one looked up. The clock ticked, and I felt that urge to go back to bed and go to sleep which is such a familiar part of the ordeal of staying with someone. The purpose goes out of life when faced with wondering whether to go and see if your bedroom's still there, or sit looking out of the window with an old copy of *Country Life*.

I must say, when it comes to not having any washing up to do, people find some pretty strange occupations to fill in their time. Killing becomes a major pre-occupation. Not content with leaving the birds and the hares and the rabbits to get on with their business of going tweet tweet and lollop lollop, they have to blast their heads off. One minute there they are lolloping and chirping about, and the next minute they're a mess, and everyone's counting them, and hanging them up, and falling over themselves to eat them once they've gone bad. And what is so baffling is the way they carry on just as if it's not happening. It's just bang-bang and 'My deah he didn't.' No qualms as it were. No perhaps I could fill in my time with something more constructive. Question mark, question mark. Of course, everyone has their theories. Most of the time I try not to have, but it does occur to you that it must be all about being afraid to die. You know, power over life and death. And when you see a rabbit with its brains splattered all over the grass it makes you feel more alive, more certain you're still there. Possibly even a trifle death-proof.

Perhaps being 'Conshies' as Julian Fashist-Pigge put it so delicately, perhaps not wanting to step outside and partake in some harmless destruction gave Clever Drawers and I too much pause for thought. We spent the morning contemplating some rose bushes, and realizing that while there is no doubt of the need to Get Out and Find Out, at the same time the reason you very rarely do, is that you don't like what you Find Out once you've Got Out.

The Pop did not come down to lunch, so we ate alone with Lady Thyng. It felt like being kept in from games to do homework. Or being in quarantine. She avoided all topics of conversation, a practice which amounts to genius in some women. Afterwards you wonder how they managed to achieve it, but at the time you are aware only that the air is filled with verbal reactions.

'How wonderful.'

'How clever.'

'Such fun.'

Whenever I say things like that to people, they look at me for a long time, or they narrow their eyes to try and see what I really mean, or they give a hollow laugh. I hate hollow laughs, they make me wish I'd never got up. This sort of thing doesn't happen to people like Lady Thyng. People don't pin people like Lady Thyng in corners and shout 'And what do you really mean?', or 'Tell me your exact definition of clever.' They accept what comes out of the mouths of blonde coiffured ladies as a matter of course, and not only as a matter of course, they actually like them to say 'How Clever', and 'Such Fun'. Clever Drawers loves it. He gets that soft 'Tell me more' look which is so unlike him. And what is so unfair is if I say 'How clever', or Such fun' he tells me not to be inane. And you can see that you might need to be blonde and coiffured and elegant in order to say such things, and what men find adorable in someone blonde and elegant, they can find repulsive in someone small and tufty.

It's like Clever Drawers. He can say a lot of things to women that they wouldn't take from anyone else, because he wears glasses, and even when he's being seriously rude they don't believe it. He was being seriously rude to Lady Thyng over lunch, but she was loving it. He was questioning things. He's always questioning things, people who've been educated tend to. Anyway, by the time coffee arrived, Lady Thyng was purring and offering to lend him her hairpiece so that he could look a really wild revolutionary. She thought her hairpiece would really suit him. What she forgot about being a revolutionary is that you can't wear tinted spectacles. I mean the idea of a whole lot of barefooted revolutionaries wearing Easy-Rider glasses detracts from the seriousness of the situation. It tends to add a levity to the idea of protest, which is not in keeping.

Clever Drawers abandoned his glasses in our room.

'Will you be able to see to eat?' I asked him as we went downstairs.

'Of course,' he said crossly, because he'd just tripped up over my knitting wool, and anyway I always irritate him by asking him where he can see *to*.

The trouble with fancy dress is that once you've made your entrance, and everyone's had a good laugh about what you look like in someone else's hairpiece with your teeth blacked out, you're left feeling like yesterday's lettuce. Somehow, the requirement of fancy dress is that you should behave all evening like you did when you first came in. You should snarl and grimace, instead of handing out olives and saying 'Gosh how super.'

'What's your knitting for?' asked Thyng.

'They used to knit while they watched the heads dropping off.'

'Oh yes. So they did. Well done, well done,' he said this to a Karl Marx who had just come in. 'I keep having to tell everyone I'm Rasputin,' he complained. 'No one seems to realize what Rasputin looked like. Do you know, this belonged to my Grandfather? I'm exactly his build. Feel this material.'

'Fantastic.'

'It is fantastic, isn't it?'

'Absolutely.'

'I like your other half's get-up. Never realized he had such good legs. Ever been in a chorus line has he?'

He walked off, and I sat down. Mr Moulded Chiffon joined me.

'Had a bloody good day's shootin', you know,' he spread himself out on the sofa. 'Bloody good. God this corset's killing me.'

He shifted uneasily in his emerald green evening dress.

'Was all Diana's damned idea. Sexual Revolution. I don't know. Just makes a change to see her with a moustache instead of lipstick on her teeth.'

'I think you look – '

'Pretty dainty, eh? I've got quite nice ankles. Used to play a lot of girls at school. Rotten luck – half the time you ended up with a black eye blubbing in the gym. Still, did you a lot of good I suppose.'

He yawned and pushed his wig back.

'Haven't had such a good day's shooting in ages. There are a lot of people down from London for this thing, you know. Thyng said Lady had asked a lot of people down from London. The Forums are meant to be coming. He's supposed to be a woman you know. I don't believe it of course, I think it's a lot of damned nonsense, but Diana says – Mind you, everything's upside down nowadays. You can't tell who's who. Will you excuse me a minute? Must just get some toppers.'

He wandered off, the hem of his gown trailing across the floor.

I got up, and started to look intent. It's a habit I have at

216

parties. If you look intent, as if you're looking for something or someone, you invariably get stopped.

'Can I be of any assistance?'

I couldn't smile back at Karl Marx because my teeth were blacked out.

'I mean to say you look as if you've lost something,' he continued. 'Can't stand about watching someone tripping all over the place on her own like this.'

I gave an enigmatic leer, or perhaps more accurately, a toothless smile. I hadn't wanted to black my teeth out, but Clever Drawers' enthusiasm had swept me along with him, and while it was all right for people like him with enough élan to carry it off, it's very difficult for persons without such assets to do anything more than try out their best Gioconda smile, and hope there will be time before dinner to rub the mascara off the ivories. There wasn't.

Dinner was laid in several rooms. Karl Marx and I were on the same table, together with two other French and several Sexual Revolutionaries, and a Wheel. Mrs Moulded Chiffon was one of the Sexual Revolutionaries. She kept feeding the Wheel his soup.

'I suppose you never thought Wheels had to eat, gosh how funny,' she shouted through her moustache.

'What on earth made you come as a Wheel?' asked Karl Marx.

'I don't know. My wife said something about it was the first revolution – you know, the wheel and that sort of thing. And that started everything rolling. She's a bit highbrow.'

'Must be bloody uncomfortable.'

'It is. Trouble is, she got me into it, and now I can't get out. Knew what she was doing if you ask me.'

'Gosh what fun!' screamed Mrs Moulded Chiffon. 'Do you want any more croutons?'

'No, and would you mind not shoving that spoon halfway down the back of my throat?'

The Wheel looked disagreeably at Mrs Moulded Chiffon, but a hint was as good as a crack over the head to her.

It occurred to me the fifth time I disentangled my foot from that of Karl Marx that he might be taking the idea of communistic living a little too seriously. It's a big moment in a person's life wondering when to bare your blackened teeth at a chap. It's the sort of thing that needs a lot of thought. Idly picking the banana out of my fruit salad, I realized that this was exactly the sort of thing that was meant to happen to people at parties. Parties are designed so that people can wrap their feet around you. The extra something that is demanded of you is a quality of give and take, an ability to play along and know exactly what's what. If you haven't got this ability, there's not much point in hoping you have. Much better to bare your teeth, as Worcester says, and potter about on your own.

I have been an habitual potterer at parties ever since I went to my first, and spent most of the evening talking to the dog. I can tell you the names on most of the porcelains in most of the houses I've visited. They are something that becomes ingrained into the memory if you spend long enough pottering in and out of cloakrooms. The names of porcelains are not to be despised. What better way of learning new words than through the study of such significant objects? 'Shanks Vitreous China.' The sheer intellectual involvement of that word 'Vitreous' is enough to idle away many long hours. The names of porcelains are to the cloakroom potterer what old photographs under the dressing table glass are to the Nose Powderer, and both know at exactly what point to emerge and look as if they've been at the party all the time.

You notice things when you've been a cloakroom potterer re-emerging in order to mingle once more with the throng. You notice that people shrink as the evening grows longer. The more they mingle and throng, the smaller they seem to become. The man who started out the evening stiffly raising his gin to his nose, will be seen bending earnestly at half mast over a decline of decolletage, who herself had started out as the epitome of corseted propriety but is now feebly trying to light the wrong end of her cigarette.

What is going on with whom is another thing that can confuse the cloakroom potterer. Whereas you may be confident that Julian Fashist-Pigge has just made a lunge at Kate at one point of the evening, you can be completely confounded when it turns out that he has mistaken one of the Pop for Lady Thyng, and they were last seen dancing in and out of the fir trees in an ecstasy of delight.

I had arranged to meet Clever Drawers by the steps. On the way I passed Mrs Moulded Chiffon slumped on a stone bench. 'I am a camera. I am a camera,' she kept saying, but she looked more like Mrs Moulded Chiffon slumped on a bench.

The light was perfect. That grey white turning into morning light that reminds you of crushed flowers and smudged mascara.

Clever Drawers was late, and I saw by the way he was limping that he had taken in more than the architect's plan of the house. It can take a chap quite some time to catch his breath when he's limping. He kept looking over his shoulder and saying 'Oh my God', in that rather annoying way people have when they know they've got something Really Interesting to tell you, and they can force you to wait for as long as they like.

'You won't believe this,' he said. He always says that when he knows I'm going to. 'We'll have to leave,' was the next thing. 'We'll have to leave before something happens.'

My mind ran quickly over the possibilities of what could happen. We could run out of small talk. That would be fairly serious. But Clever Drawers was looking extremely shifty. Could they have discovered the cake tin under the bed? The biscuits in the sponge bag? Were we going to face social disgrace on account of an unnatural predilection for fruit cake? Would it even filter through to the Press? 'Lord Thyng denies Fruit Cake Orgy.' Dot dot, dot.

'Listen. Don't talk to me about him,' Clever Drawers groaned.

You have to say 'Why not?' when people say things like that. You have to say – quickly – 'Why' and 'What happened' and 'Why don't you want me to talk to you about Thyng.' Question mark, question mark. And then you find out things like he's bent, and he's always fancied Clever Drawers, and so has she, so they thought they'd share him, just like a piece of fruit cake. Exclamation mark.

'I wondered why he kept saying you had such wonderful legs,' I said perceptively.

I hadn't of course, I hadn't wondered once why Thyng had

said what wonderful legs he had, but you always say things like that when you don't want to seem taken aback.

'Congratulations,' I added. 'You could have brought off the Spring Double.'

'Shut up. I'm not staying here. With them. They could have raped me.'

We went up the stairs to our room. On the way we passed one of the Pop who was bending earnestly over the hall table, intent on inscribing it. Later, as we passed him once more, our suitcases in our hands, he was leaning back, admiring the fruits of his industry. In the middle of the fine table, where before had been virgin wood, he had just carved 'Make Love Not War.'

10

Actually, now I'm here, I can't say I like endings very much either. I used to think they were rather good, and spent a lot of time putting 'Fin', and 'Tigy-Sur-Loire, 1963' at the bottom of things. The temptation is still there, but somehow '215 Staithe Avenue' hasn't the same ring, and if you put a date people spend the rest of your life counting backwards and saying 'She Must Be At Least Sixty' – which could be bad news if you were only fifty-nine.

Of course, finishing something is always the same. Glowing notices floating in front of the eyes, hours spent grappling with the problem of what to ask for the film rights. And then later, reality hovering in the shape of other people making Useful Remarks.

'I thought that bit worked *very* well.'

A sudden rush of pleasure to the head, and then:

'Which bit?' And: 'What's wrong with the other bits?'

Still, to finish something is after all not nothing. It usually means you feel quite amiable towards your fellow creatures, distinctively more affable, as if you've just deposited a heavy suitcase at the Left Luggage.

Now you can do all those things you've been looking forward to doing. You can lie in bed without page nine floating in front of your eyes, you can listen to the constant drip of your neighbour's overflow without being reminded of Man's Lot, and you can pick up where you left off, before you wrote 'Chapter One', 'Page One'. Dot dot, dot.

Except – you can never quite remember what it was you were doing before. Of course when you remember, you will have no hesitation in taking whatever it was up again, it's just that until you do, there seems very little point in going back to it.

Whereas, on the other hand, it just so happens that a little some-thing occurred to you the other day which seems worth noting.

And now you come to mention it, that noise of the neigh-bour's overflow – that constant drip, drip, drip. It really is very reminiscent of Man's Lot. No honestly.

More about Penguins and Pelicans